D1249144

THE LORD'S PRAYER

Our Father in heaven,
hallowed be your name,
your kingdom come,
your will be done
on earth as in heaven.
Give us today our daily bread.
Forgive us our sins
as we forgive those who sin against us.
And lead us not into temptation,
but deliver us from evil.
For the kingdom, the power,
and the glory are yours
now and for ever. Amen.

BE OUR FREEDOM, LORD

Responsive Prayers and Readings For Contemporary Worship

Prepared and edited by Terry C. Falla

GRAND RAPIDS, MICHIGAN
WILLIAM B. EERDMANS PUBLISHING COMPANY

This American edition published 1984 through
special arrangement with Lutheran Publishing House by
Wm. B. Eerdmans Publishing Company,
255 Jefferson S.E., Grand Rapids, Mich. 49503

Library of Congress Cataloging in Publication Data

Main entry under title:
Be our freedom, Lord.

   Reprint. Originally published: Adelaide, S. Aust. :
Lutheran Pub. House, c1981.
   Includes index.
   1. Prayer-books. 2. Meditations. I. Falla,
Terry C., 1940-   .
BV245.B49   1984   264'.13   84-10339

ISBN 0-8028-0014-9

To Ailsa Moot
without whose devotion and dedication
to the task of typing the manuscripts
of four very different editions
and countless revisions
this book would never have reached
the point of publication.

I acknowledge with affection and gratitude the contributions
of the many people whose help, suggestions, and encouragement
led to the creation of this book.

Especially I wish to record my gratitude to:

Berris
Adele Davies
Peter Dyson
Llew Evans
Allison Forbes
Jill Francis
Graeme Garrett
Athol Gill
Jos. Goudswaard
Ray Gribble
Robert Gribbon
Sandra Groome
Vickie Guthrie
Ian Hansen
Helen Hoffman
Cherry Jackson
Judith Jones
Mike Kellock
Ross Langmead
Everard Leske
Myles Lynch
Jenny Marr
Rex O'Brien
Pam Oliver
Vicki Paunkov
Frank Rees
Bruce Rumbold
Jean Rumbold
Lillian Russell
Alan Wade
Jan Wade
Roy Walshe
The Rosanna Baptist Church, where in
our work and worship together the
tentative use of a few responsive prayers
and readings composed by members of the
congregation grew into an adventure,
became a book, and then a journey —
and for other reasons altogether,
Bruce M. Metzger.

POINT OF DEPARTURE

In its creation over a long period of time, this book
has become much more than a collection of prayers.
It is a journal, a journey, a pilgrimage. It is an
affirmation of faith, a call to freedom, an invitation
to joy. While each prayer and reading can be used in
its own right, it is also part of a whole that develops
a theme, has rhythm and movement, and tells a
story.

The origins of the prayers and readings are as
diverse as they are different, and come from every
part of our globe. Some were written in the confines
of a prison cell, others in the context of a caring
community; some in the midst of suffering and
poverty, others during days of creative solitude.
Some come to us from the distant past and link us
with those whose journey we continue; others are not
only contemporary, but look to a future fraught with
unprecedented fears and limitless possibilities.

But whoever the authors and whatever the
circumstances, together they voice the praises,
laments, confessions, and commitment of the people
of God; they express the struggles, the hopes, the
fears, and the faith of a pilgrim people: the mystery
of our existence, our experiences of desolation and
darkness, our infinite longings, and our need for a
faith that transcends the anxieties of the present,
confronts us with the evil and injustices of our day,
and points us to the horizons of God's purpose and
love.

As a prayer book, *Be Our Freedom, Lord* is not
intended to replace any liturgy, but to provide
resources for community worship and personal
reflection.

As a worship book, it calls for the participation of
the whole congregation, and frequently allows for
more than one reader to lead the people. This is often
most effective when the voices are male and female.
A change of reader is indicated by placing • at the
beginning of a stanza for the first reader, •• for
the second, and ••• when there is a third.

Inevitably, any such book will always have its dangers. All too often the prayers we say become just so many words recited without meaning or any intention of acting upon them. For this reason, our own and each succeeding generation demand the rediscovery of the purpose and place of responsive prayers and litanies in our worship, and written prayers in our personal meditation. To do this, we could find no better starting-point than the Bible itself.

When we consider the prayers recorded in the Scriptures: the prayers of Jeremiah and Job, those brought together in the Psalms, and those scattered throughout the New Testament, we find that for those who composed them, whether they intended them for public worship or private use, prayer was a process, a process that required looking back, reflecting, thinking, seeking, searching, and, above all, listening and responding.

Prayers for worship, no less than the 'prayer of stillness', require reaching out to our innermost self, to our fellow human beings, and to God.[1] Prayer changes our vision of the world and so influences our actions in it.[2]

Of course, no prayer in this or any other book can generate the awareness of the living Lord which the Holy Spirit alone can give; but, as we work and worship together, they can at least open a way by which we allow the Spirit to enter.[3]

1. Henri J.M. Nouwen, *Reaching Out*, Collins Fount Paperbacks, 1976.
2. John Macquarrie, *Paths in Spirituality*, SCM Press Ltd., 1972, chapter III.
3. John V. Taylor, *The Go-Between God*, SCM Press Ltd., chapter 11.

THE WAY AHEAD

Moments on the way 11

PART ONE
Invocation and call to worship 19
Affirmation of faith 41

PART TWO
Call and commission 57
Praise and thanksgiving 67
Lament 83
Confession and forgiveness...................... 97
Intercession 117
Offering.. 151
Commitment 163
Celebration 175

PART THREE
Advent.. 199
Christmas....................................... 209
Year's end and new year 219
Epiphany 223
Lent 237
Passiontide 259
Good Friday..................................... 263
Easter 271
Pentecost....................................... 277

PART FOUR
Welcoming 287
Commissioning 293
Parting 301

PART FIVE
Meditations for a pilgrim people 313

INDEXES
Prayers especially suitable for children 356
Titles in alphabetical order 356
Authors and sources.............................
Scripture passages ....

MOMENTS ON THE WAY

PART ONE

INVOCATION AND CALL TO WORSHIP

Here and now 20
Summons to praise 21
The call of freedom has been sounded 21
Praise him, all creation 22
Good news for celebration 23
Called to serve the cause of right 23
Worship without pretence 24
Your word and your truth in our midst 25
Testing the promise by living the hope 25
Mercy and freedom are his gifts 26
Our utmost need 27
Though the mountains may depart 28
The immense longing 29
Where many paths and errands meet 30
Because you believe in us 32
Pervade us, O God, with your presence 33
Widely as his mercy flows 34
Attune us to your silence 34
To make your purpose our purpose 35
Come away 35
Let the winds of the Spirit 36
Maker of heaven and earth 37
Acclaim with joy the depths of his love 38
I have called you by name 39
Praise for the past and trust for the future 39
Gloria in excelsis 40

AFFIRMATION OF FAITH

Alpha and Omega 42
There is a new world 43
The cosmic Christ 44
Life can begin again 46
The meaning of providence 48
When the seas rage and mountains fall 49
God's everlasting kindness 50
Risen and still with you 52

PART TWO

CALL AND COMMISSION

Our call and commission 58
The community of grace 61
Our mission in the world 63
The goad of the promised future 66

PRAISE AND THANKSGIVING

Alive! 68
We do not take an untravelled way 69
Joy comes in the morning 71
Your love is strong enough 72
Patience that waits our returning 73
Thanks for our heritage 74
Recognizing the bonds 75
Fun times 76
Of driving clouds and open skies 77
Grass by the roadside 78
Lord of the storm............................. 79
The earth is yours 80
In awe and welcome stand 81
Cosmic hymn of praise 82

LAMENT

Out of the depths............................. 84
Broken bones may joy......................... 85
My days are in your hand 86
Things that make me sad....................... 87
He is hidden 88
Shafts of trust................................ 89
Longing for tomorrow and losing today 90
Rebellion..................................... 92
A people on trial 94
Eternal God and mortal man 96

CONFESSION AND FORGIVENESS

A plea for God's forgiveness 98
I have betrayed 98
If I flew to the point of sunrise 99
Jesus... 100
You shall know the truth 102
Beyond all pretence 103
Put your name upon us.......................... 104
Father, forgive 105
We give you what we are 106
Free to forget our pride 107

11

The times we talk too much 108
Power 109
Tensed against tenderness........................ 110
Blindness 112
Participants in evil 113
Failed 114
Penitence 115
Take fire 116

INTERCESSION

A prayer of Ignatius Loyola 118
Steps marking our way 119
Enough!.. 120
That dreams may be dreamt 121
The divine discontent........................... 122
The promise of your presence 123
In all things be our strength.................... 124
A letter not written with ink 125
To know God is to do justice 126
The Word was made flesh 127
God saw all that he had made 128
Every part of our life 130
Courage to change 132
Limb and mind in harmony 133
Sharing 134
Many lovely things............................. 134
God gives 134
Belonging 135
Make us healthy-minded........................ 136
Go with us, Lord 137
Forbid! 138
Love which leads to awareness 139
For our city and ourselves 140
A litany for the Lucky Country 142
A world in which faith comes hard 144
When in prison you came to my cell 145
But not alone.................................... 147
The unquenchable hope 149
Peace prayer of Francis of Assisi 150

OFFERING

With what gifts shall we come before him?....... 152
Whatsoever you do 153
Find your love 154
Where your treasure is.......................... 155
Counterfeit?..................................... 156
Against the wind................................ 156
The rhythm of community 158

Never too poor to be generous.................... 159
Using our gifts 159
Yours is the kingdom............................ 160
We commit ourselves to live in love 160
Messengers of hope............................... 161
Bread with laughter 162

COMMITMENT

Venturing the harder road....................... 164
Liberty to the oppressed 166
Redemptive suffering 168
Between already and not yet..................... 170
Our ultimate loyalty............................. 172
Come, Lord 174

CELEBRATION

Granting of forgiveness 177
The scandal of grace 178
Given for the life of the world................... 180
We are your family 180
Just as we are.................................... 181
We share his peace 182
Do this, remembering me 182
Brought together to break bread 184
The thanksgiving 186
You have met us in your Son 189
Sounds of the Sacrament 190
The pledge of the Spirit......................... 193
Dreams for celebration 194

PART THREE

ADVENT

Tomorrows filled with promise................... 200
Mary's song...................................... 201
The insatiable desire 202
Dawn for our darkness 204
He is one of us 205
To receive your gift.............................. 206
The rainbow of our future 208

CHRISTMAS

Emmanuel 210
Surprised by joy................................. 212
Christmastide profiles 214
The grace unspeakable 215

Hallelujah for the Christ-child! 216
Robert Louis Stevenson's
    Christmas Day prayer 218

YEAR'S END AND NEW YEAR

Year's end 220
New Year 221

EPIPHANY

Beyond what the silent stars tell 224
Light of the world 226
You are accepted 228
A surprising start 230
The morning sun from heaven 232
The unexpected at every turn 233
One Lord, one faith, one hope 234

LENT

Where the Spirit of the Lord is, there is
    freedom 236
The simplicity of the carefree life 238
Choices 240
The cost of discipleship 241
The true wilderness 242
Temptation 244
Vision and mirage 246
Doing the truth 248
Forgiveness 250
The new commandment 251
Shadows of fear 253
The darkness is never so distant 254
When little is left 256
The threshold 257
To the end 258

PASSIONTIDE

Who takes away the sin of the world 260
Jesus our Lord 260
The centre of the mystery of the Christ 262

GOOD FRIDAY

Ours were the sorrows he carried 264
The safest response to the surprising God? 266
Good Friday 268
Forsaken? 269
Delivered to death for our misdeeds 270

EASTER

Confessions at the empty tomb 272
Healings from the empty tomb 274
Crucified risen one! 275
Through the flames of heaven 276

PENTECOST

More than we can measure or imagine 278
Breath of our life 279
Lord of the winds and fires of earth 280
In the stillness 281
Powers beyond our own 282
The wind of the Spirit 283

PART FOUR

WELCOMING

The open church 288
A gift of grace................................... 290
Children learn what they live.................... 291
The blessing of a child 292

COMMISSIONING

Induction of elders or deacons 294
Induction of teachers or leaders................. 296
The commitment of the community 298
I lift my eyes to the hills........................ 299
Go well, stay well 300

PARTING

Glimpses of a winding road 302
Strength to comfort 303
To your safe keeping 304
Letting go....................................... 305
Valley of the shadow 306
Your love is stronger than death................. 308
Footprints on the shore.......................... 309

PART FIVE

MEDITATIONS FOR A PILGRIM PEOPLE

A taste of sawdust and a thirst for truth 314
Gossip 317
Holiness 320
Transformed nonconformist 322
Fortitude.. 326
Happiness is 328
Love's as warm as tears 335
Step into joy 338

Footnote to all prayers 356

1

Invocations and calls to worship

I did not come to call the virtuous,
but sinners.

Jesus

Here and now

This is the place
and this is the time;
here and now God waits
to break into
our experience:

To change our minds,
to change our lives,
to change our ways;

To make us see the world
and the whole of life
in a new light;

To fill us with hope,
joy, and certainty
for the future.

This is the place,
as are all places;
this is the time,
as are all times.

Here and now,
let us praise him.

Summons to praise Psalm 117

Praise the Lord, all nations!
Extol him, all peoples!

For great is his steadfast love toward us;
the Lord's faithfulness endures for ever.

Then let us praise the Lord.

The call of freedom has been sounded

Jesus our Lord is risen.

Lord, may we experience
the power of your resurrection
and live by it.

The call of freedom
has been sounded.

Lord, may we respond
as the community of the free.

It concerns every one of us personally,
in our place, in our humanity,
in this world of ours.

Lord, may the spirit and gift of your freedom
break the spell of our fears and send us away
obedient rebels, lovers of life's depths,
and your disciples for ever. Amen.

Praise him, all creation Psalm 96

Sing a new song to the Lord.
Sing to the Lord all the earth.
Sing to the Lord, bless his name.

Proclaim his salvation day by day,
tell his glory among the nations,
tell his marvels to every people.

The Lord himself made the heavens,
in his presence are splendour and majesty,
in his sanctuary power and beauty.

Ascribe to the Lord, families of the people,
ascribe to the Lord beauty and power,
ascribe to the Lord the glory due to his name.

Bring an offering, bear it before him,
worship the Lord in the splendour of holiness,
tremble before him, all the earth!

Let the heavens rejoice and the earth be glad,
let the sea thunder and all that it holds,
let the fields exult and all that is in them,
let all the trees of the forest cry out for joy,

At the presence of the Lord, for he comes,
he comes to rule the earth,
to judge the world with justice
and the nations with his truth.

Good news for celebration

The work of the Creator is visible:
Let us respond with praise.

The example of Jesus is apparent:
Let us respond with obedience.

The wind of the Spirit is blowing:
Let us respond with joy.

The word of God is calling:
Let us worship in spirit and in truth.

Called to serve the cause of right Isaiah 42:5-7

Thus says God, the Eternal One,
he who created the heavens
and spread them out,
who gave shape to the earth
and what comes from it,
who gave life to its people
and the creatures that move in it:

I, the Eternal, have called you
to serve the cause of right;
I have taken you by the hand
and formed you.

I have appointed you
as a covenant of the people
and a light of the nations,
to open the eyes of the blind,
to free captives from prison,
and those who live in darkness
from the dungeon.

Lord, help us fulfil
our calling. Amen.

Worship without pretence   Romans 12:1,2, 9-13

Think of God's mercy, my fellow disciples,
and worship him, I beg you,
in a way that is worthy of thinking beings,
by offering your living bodies as a holy sacrifice,
truly pleasing to God.

*Do not model yourselves
on the behaviour of the world around you,
but let your behaviour change,
modelled by your new mind.*

This is the only way
to discover the will of God
and know what is good,
what it is that God wants,
what is the perfect thing to do.

*Do not let your love be a pretence,
but sincerely prefer good to evil.
Love each other as true friends
and have a profound respect for each other.*

Work for the Lord with untiring effort
and with great earnestness of spirit.
If you have hope, this will make you cheerful.
Do not give up if trials come, and keep on praying.

*If any of your fellow travellers are in need,
you must share with them;
and you should make hospitality
your special care.*

Your word and your truth in our midst

We praise you, our Father,
for making your divine truth
real to us in Jesus Christ.

We ask that what we do,
how we live, and the way we love,
may increasingly become
a worthy response.

Amen.

Testing the promise by living the hope

Jesus promises a new freedom
within a new commitment:
'This do and you shall live.'
We test the promise by letting our life
express the hope that it will be kept.

O Lord Christ, help us this day and every day
to maintain ourselves in simplicity and in joy:
the joy of the merciful, the joy of genuine love,
the joy of all who hunger and thirst for justice.

Grant that, by renouncing henceforth
all thought of looking back,
and joyful with infinite gratitude,
we may never fear to precede the dawn,

To praise,
        to bless,
                and sing
                        to Christ our Lord.

Amen.

Mercy and freedom are his gifts

CALL TO WORSHIP

The Lord be with you.
And also with you.
O come let us worship the Eternal,
for he is our Father.
Let us praise him,
for he is our Creator, Lord, and Redeemer.

He is our God,
and we are his people,
whom he has called to serve the cause of right:
to bring good news to the poor,
to proclaim liberty to prisoners,
and recovery of sight for the blind,
to set the downtrodden free,
*to proclaim the year of the Lord's favour.**

INVOCATION

RESPONSE

We praise you, Creator, our Father:
we acknowledge your control over the world.

We confess ourselves believers who have sinned:
we come to you forgiving one another.

Reassure us of forgiveness.
Reassure us of your presence.

Re-engage us in your service:
because of Jesus Christ our Lord. Amen.

* Luke 4:18

Our utmost need

God our Father, and Lord of all being,
we do not rely on our own good deeds,
but on your great mercy,
as we lay our needs before you.

For what are we?
What is our life?
What is our love?

What is our justice?
What is our success?
What is our endurance?
What is our power?

Lord, hear! Lord, pardon!
Lord, listen and act!

Lord, be for us the truth on which
life and death are built,
the hope that cannot be destroyed,
the freedom from which love and justice flow,
and the joy that has eternity within it.

Amen.

Though the mountains may depart

Thus says the Lord, who created you,
who formed you in the womb,
who is your help:

Do not be afraid, do not be dismayed,
with tender affection I will bring you back home;
you are mine, I will never forget you.

The mountains may depart, the hills be shaken,
but my love for you will never leave you;
with a love that is everlasting do I love you.

Your faults I have dispelled like a cloud,
your sins like a mist. Come back to me,
for I have redeemed you.

Then seek the Lord while he is still to be found,
call to him while he is still near.

Let the wicked man abandon his way,
the evil man his thoughts.

Let him turn back to the Lord who will take pity
on him, to our God who is rich in forgiving.

For my thoughts are not your thoughts,
my ways not your ways.

Yes, the heavens are as high above earth
as my ways are above your ways, my thoughts
above your thoughts — it is the Lord who speaks.

Isaiah 43:1; 44:2,21,22;
54:4,7,8,10; 55:6-9.

The immense longing

Eternal God, we come, we come again,
seeking, hoping, wanting to hear your word.

*We come because, despite our best efforts,
we have failed to live by bread alone.*

We come impelled by a desire too deep for words,
with longings that are too infinite to express.

*We come yearning for meaning in our existence
and purpose for our life.*

We come acknowledging our need for each other's
affirmation and encouragement, understanding and love.

*We come confessing our dependence on you.
Lord, embrace us with your forgiveness, and claim us
by the mystery and depths of your love.*

Amen.

Where many paths and errands meet

O Lord, our God!
You know who we are:

People with a good conscience,
people with a bad conscience,

Happy people and unhappy people,
reassured and anxious,

Christians by conviction or tradition,
believers, half-believers, and unbelievers.

And you know from where we come:
from warmth of home or icy loneliness,

From parents, friends, acquaintances,
or from a great solitude,

From a peaceful background
or from all sorts of difficulties and torments,

From family circumstances which are happy
or tense or broken;

From the heart of the Christian community
or from its periphery.

Here we are before you
in spite of our differences:

All equal by the fact
that we have wronged you and each other,

Equal because we all must die,
equal because we would be lost without your grace,

Equal also because your grace is promised and given to us in your dear Son, our Lord Jesus Christ.

We are gathered together to praise you
and to let you speak to us.

May it be so during this time we have together
and the week of work ahead of us.

For we ask it in the name
and by the words of your Son:

Our Father in heaven,
hallowed be your name,
your kingdom come,
your will be done,
on earth as in heaven.
Give us today our daily bread.
Forgive us the wrong we have done,
as we have forgiven those who have wronged us.
And lead us not into temptation,
but deliver us from evil.

For yours is the kingdom,
the power and the glory,
now and for ever. Amen.

Because you believe in us

Almighty God, we your creatures
need to be won again and again
for your church and your kingdom.

We have promised —
and we have betrayed you.
We have offered you our loyalty —
and withdrawn it again.

We are men and women
in whom splendour and shame
are strangely mixed.
Yet we return ever and anon,
for we cannot keep away from you.

You have the words of eternal life;
to whom then can we go but to you?
We are here today,
not because we believe in you,
but because you believe in us.

Help us to stand in that faith.
We ask this in the name of your Son,
Jesus Christ our Lord.

Amen.

Pervade us, O God, with your presence

Lord God,
we have come to worship you
as sinners in need of your forgiveness.

*We come tired from our work,
in need of refreshment and recreation.*

We come with worries,
in need of your guidance.

*But first, please lift us
out of our preoccupation
with our own needs.*

Allow us to see you
with the eyes of faith,
and to hear with understanding
what you say to us.

*Make us thankful
for all the good
we have received from you.*

Awaken in us a longing
to do what is right.

*And make us aware
of the great company,
past, present, and to come,
with whom we join
to worship you.
Amen.*

Widely as his mercy flows

Almighty and everlasting God,
always more ready to hear
than we to pray,
and to give more
than either we desire or deserve,

Pour down upon us
the abundance of your mercy,

Forgiving us those things
of which our conscience is afraid,

And giving us those good things
which we are not worthy to ask.

Through Jesus Christ,
your Son, our Lord.

Amen.

Attune us to your silence

You wait for us
until we are open to you.

We wait for your word
to make us receptive.

Attune us to your voice,
to your silence.

Speak and bring your Son to us —
Jesus, the word of your peace.

To make your purpose our purpose

By your word, Lord God,
you set free everyone
imprisoned in himself.

To freedom you have called us
to become men and women
in the image and the spirit
of Jesus Christ.

Our Father,
give us the strength
that his life has first provided,
and the openness that he has
prepared for us.

Make us receptive and free, so that
with you we may live for this world.
Amen.

Come away

O Lord Jesus Christ,
who said to your disciples,
'Come away by yourselves and rest awhile':

Grant us to seek you
whom our souls desire to love;

That we may both find you
and be found by you;

Who with the Father,
in the unity of the Spirit,
lives and reigns,

God: our Creator, Lord, and Redeemer,
for ever and ever.

Amen.

Let the winds of the Spirit

We worship, praise, and adore you,
our Creator, Lord, and Redeemer.
We worship you, poignantly aware
that man's days are measured, that
'no longer than a wild flower he lives,
one gust of wind and he is gone'.

But we also worship as creatures
'whom you have made a little lower than the gods,
whom you have crowned with glory and honour'.
Within us you have put the whisper of eternity;
you have spiced our dreams with stardust —
and we cannot escape you.

In you, Eternal Father,
and through your Son Jesus Christ,
we find the beginning and end of all things.
In him we find hope, forgiveness,
and the courage for new beginnings.

Let then, O God,
the fresh winds of your Spirit
sweep into our lives this day,
so that this act of worship
and the week to follow
may become a time of renewal
and rededication to your service.
Amen.

Quotations from Psalms 103 & 8

Maker of heaven and earth

Who was it measured the water of the sea
in the hollow of his hand
and calculated the dimensions of the heavens,
gauged the whole earth to the bushel,
weighed the mountains in scales,
the hills in a balance?

Who could have advised the spirit of the Lord,
what counsellor could have instructed him?
Whom has he consulted to enlighten him,
and to learn the path of justice,
and discover the most skilful ways?

Thus says the Lord, your redeemer,
he who formed you in the womb:

I, myself, the Lord, made all things,
I alone spread out the heavens,
and gave shape to the earth.
I am the first and the last,
there is no other God beside me.

Then come, let us worship the Eternal,
for he is our Creator, Lord, and Redeemer.
Let us praise him,
for he is our Father.
He is our God,
And we are his people,
whom he has called to serve the cause of right:
to bring good news to the poor,
to bind up hearts that are broken,
to proclaim liberty to prisoners,
and recovery of sight for the blind,
to set the downtrodden free,
to proclaim the year of the Lord's favour.

Isaiah 40:12-14; 44:6,24
Luke 4:18 quoted from Isaiah

Acclaim with joy the depths of his love

CALL TO WORSHIP

Acclaim the Lord, all the earth!
Serve the Lord gladly,
come into his presence with songs of joy!

Know that he, the Lord, is God!
It is he that made us, and we are his;
we are his people, the flock that he pastures.

Enter these doors giving thanks,
come into this place praising him,
give thanks to him, bless his name!

Yes, the Lord is good,
his love is everlasting,
his faithfulness endures from age to age. *

INVOCATION

RESPONSE

Living God,
we come to worship you,
praising you for the past
and trusting you for the future!

We come to join our will to your will,
to make your purpose our purpose,
and your love our love.

We come in the name of Jesus Christ our Lord.

Amen.

* Psalm 100

I have called you by name, you are mine

Isaiah 43:1

Acclaim the Lord, all the earth!
Serve the Lord gladly,
come into his presence with songs of joy!

Know that he, the Lord, is God!
It is he that made us, and we are his;
we are his people, the flock that he pastures.

Enter these doors giving thanks,
come into this place praising him,
give thanks to him, bless his name!

Yes, the Lord is good,
his love is everlasting,
*his faithfulness endures from age to age.**

Praise for the past and trust for the future

Living God,
we come to worship you,
praising you for the past
and trusting you for the future!

We come to join our will to your will,
to make your purpose our purpose,
and your love our love.

We come in the name of Jesus Christ our Lord.

Amen.

* Psalm 100

Gloria in excelsis

Glory to God in the highest,
and peace to his people on earth.

Lord God, heavenly King,
almighty God and Father,
we worship you, we give you thanks,
we praise you for your glory.

Lord Jesus Christ, only Son of the Father,
Lord God, Lamb of God,
you take away the sin of the world:
have mercy on us;
you are seated at the right hand of the Father:
receive our prayer.

For you alone are the Holy One;
you alone are the Lord;
you alone are the Most High,
Jesus Christ, with the Holy Spirit,
in the glory of God the Father.
Amen.

Affirmation of faith

The Gospel is that God's love can be trusted
absolutely and cannot be destroyed.

Daniel Day Williams

For other prayers and readings which
may be used as affirmations of faith,
see those entitled:

Though the mountains may
  depart 28
Joy comes in the morning 71
Your love is strong enough 72
Steps marking our way 119
Enough! 120
You are accepted 228
A surprising start 230
The morning sun from heaven . 232

One Lord, one faith, one hope .. 234
The new commandment 251
Jesus our Lord 260
The centre of the mystery of
  the Christ..................... 262
Ours were the sorrows he carried 264
The wind of the Spirit 283
Glimpses of a winding road 302
Love's as warm as tears 335

Alpha and Omega

- Before galaxies burned in empty night,
  planets hurled through deepest space,
  waves broke upon primeval shores,
  volcanoes roared with molten rock;

  Before lightning split an angry sky,
  glaciers cut through tortured steeps,
  flowers danced in zephyr winds,
  streams chattered by forest glades,

  You were already God.

  And when in unimagined aeons
  the earth ignites in flames of dying sun;
  or missiles flash to cities doomed,
  ash drifts, boughs break, unheard, unseen,

  You will still be God.

- ● Christ risen, what futile, cold assurance,
  if he were not *our* God! But Alpha, cosmic,
  crucified, he comes in grace confounding:
  Omega, Father, Saviour, Friend;

  Our Judge, our Breath, our Joy.

There is a new world

In human experience it is a rare thing
for someone to die for another,
though perhaps for a good person
one might actually brave death.

But Christ died for us while we were yet sinners,
and that is God's own proof of his love toward us.

His purpose in dying for all was that those who live
should no longer live for themselves,
but for him who died and was raised to life for them.

With us, therefore, worldly standards have ceased
to count in our estimate of any person.

For when anyone is united to Christ,
there is a new world!

The old order has gone, and a new order
has already begun.

It is all God's work.

He has reconciled us to himself through Christ,
and he has given us the work
of handing on this reconciliation.

In other words, God was in Christ
reconciling the world to himself,
no longer holding people's misdeeds against them.

And he has entrusted us with the news
that they are reconciled.

We come therefore as Christ's ambassadors,
and the appeal we make in Christ's name is:

Be reconciled to God.

Romans 5:7,8
2 Corinthians 5:15-21

The cosmic Christ Colossians 1:13-23

This is what he has done:
He has rescued us from the dominion of darkness
and brought us away to the kingdom of his dear Son.

And in him we gain our freedom,
the forgiveness of our sins.

He is the image of the unseen God;
his is the primacy over all created things.

In him everything in heaven
and on earth was created:

Everything visible and everything invisible,
thrones, sovereignties, authorities, and powers;

The whole universe has been created
through him and for him.

He exists before everything,
and all things are held together in him.

And now he is the head of the body
which is the Church.

He is its origin,
the first to return from the dead,
to be in all things alone supreme.

For in him the complete being of God,
by God's own choice,
came to dwell.

Through him God chose to reconcile
the whole universe to himself,
making peace through the shedding
of his blood upon the cross —

To reconcile all things,
whether on earth or in heaven,
through him alone.

You were yourselves estranged from God;
you were his enemies in heart and mind,
and your deeds were evil.

But now by Christ's death
in his body of flesh and blood
God has reconciled you to himself,
so that he may present you before himself,
dedicated, without blame or reproach.

As long, that is, as you persevere
and stand firm in the faith,

Never letting yourselves drift away
from the hope offered in the Good News
which you have heard.

This is the Gospel
which has been proclaimed
in the whole creation under heaven.

And we have become its ministers:
ambassadors of God
and the servants of his Son.

Life can begin again

● And you he made alive,
when you were dead
through the sins and wickedness
in which you once walked,
when you followed the evil ways
of this present age.

But God, who is rich in mercy,
out of the great love with which he loved us,
made us alive together with Christ
even when we were dead in our sins.

For it is by grace you are saved,
through trusting him;
it is not your own doing.

It is God's gift,
not a reward for work done.
There is nothing for anyone to boast of.

We are God's handiwork,
created in Christ Jesus
to devote ourselves to the good deeds
for which God has designed us. *

●● Most gracious God, Father of our Lord Jesus Christ,
we thank you that all our days are lived
in the presence of your eternal love.

*We thank you that to experience the reality
of your love in Jesus Christ
is to step from a living death
to life itself.*

We know, and know so well,
what it means to exist in a world
where life is not real life at all,
but a deadness of spirit —
a deadness in which the possibility
of the flowering of goodness and truth
seem to be just a wishful dream.

* Ephesians 2:1-10: selections

But, because of your steadfast love,
there is always the possibility
for life and light to enter into
our own life to transform and heal us.

We thank you that in Jesus, crucified and risen,
we see your eternal love for all people,
for those who hate you,
who turn from you, who are indifferent to you;

That you keep on loving us
even when we reject you completely;
that to you every person, every one of us,
is precious — of infinite value;

That our worth to you is not dependent
on whether we are good or bad,
on what we have done or failed to do;

That your love is total, unconditional, free,
never based on our behaviour, or accomplishments,
or capacity — that you love us because we are us.

God our Father, God of Jesus, whose love
never forces itself on us or on our world,
but waits, longing, yearning, suffering,
bearing — waiting, waiting:

We praise you that your raising Christ from the dead
is no mere doctrine or memory we must try
to defend, or re-live, or recapture,

But an act of grace and a call to freedom,
that we might share his risen life,

That we might experience, mortal though we are,
the reality of your presence and power and love,

That we might know that life can begin again.

Amen.

The meaning of providence

With all this in mind, what can we add?
With God on our side, who can be against us?

Since God did not spare his own Son,
but gave him up to benefit us all,
we may be certain, after such a gift,
that he will not refuse anything he can give.

Could anyone accuse those that God has chosen?
When God acquits, could anyone condemn?
Could Christ Jesus?

No! He not only died for us —
he rose from the dead,
and there at God's right hand
he stands and pleads for us.

Then, what can separate us
from the love of Christ?
Can trouble do it,
or hardship?

Can persecution,
or hunger, or poverty,
or danger, or death?

As Scripture says,
'For your sake we are in danger of death
the whole day long,
we are treated like sheep
that are going to be slaughtered.'

These are the trials through which we triumph,
by the power of him who loved us.

For I am convinced of this:
that there is nothing in life or death,
in the realm of spirits or superhuman powers,
in the world as it is or the world as it shall be,
in the forces of the universe,
in the heights or depths —

Nothing in all creation
that can separate us
from the love of God
in Christ Jesus our Lord.

When the seas rage and mountains fall Psalm 46

God is our refuge, our strength,
ever ready to help in time of trouble;
so we shall not fear though the earth gives way,
though the mountains fall into the depths of the sea,
though its waters roar and seethe,
and the mountains reel as they rage.

The Lord of hosts is with us,
the God of Jacob our high stronghold.

There is a river whose streams refresh the city of God,
and it sanctifies the dwelling of the Most High.
God is in that city, she will not be overthrown;
at the break of dawn he helps her.
Nations are in tumult, kingdoms hurled down,
God thunders, and the earth surges like the sea.

The Lord of hosts is with us,
the God of Jacob our high stronghold.

Come, consider the works of the Lord,
the redoubtable deeds he has done on the earth:
he brings wars to an end all over the world,
he breaks the bow, he snaps the spear,
he burns the shield in the fire.
'Be still, and know that I am God,
exalted among the nations, exalted over the earth!'

The Lord of hosts is with us,
the God of Jacob our high stronghold.

God's everlasting kindness   Psalm 103

Bless the Lord, my soul,
and all that is within me, bless his holy name.
Bless the Lord, my soul,
and remember all his kindnesses:

In forgiving all your offences,
healing all your suffering,
in redeeming your life from the depths,
crowning you with love and tenderness,
in filling your years with well-being,
renewing your youth like an eagle's.

The Lord, who does what is right,
is always on the side of the oppressed;
he revealed his intention to Moses,
what he could do to the sons of Israel.

The Lord is tender and compassionate,
slow to anger, most loving;
his indignation does not last for ever,
his anger exists a short time only;
he never treats us, never punishes us,
as our guilt and our sins deserve.

No less than the height of heaven over earth
is the greatness of his love for those who fear him;
he takes our sins farther away
than the east is from the west.

As tenderly as a father treats his children,
so the Lord treats those who love him;
he knows what we are made of,
he remembers we are dust.

Man lasts no longer than grass;
no longer than a wildflower he lives;
one gust of wind, and he is gone,
never to be seen there again.

Yet the Lord's love for those who fear him
lasts from all eternity and for ever,
like his goodness to their children's children,
as long as they keep his covenant
and remember to obey his precepts.

The Lord has established his reign in the heavens,
his power over the whole world.
Bless the Lord, all his messengers,
creatures of might who do his bidding.

Bless the Lord, all his hosts,
his ministers who serve his will.
Bless the Lord, all created things
in every part of his kingdom.
Bless the Lord, O my soul.

Risen and still with you Luke 9 and Matthew 28

- You are wayfarers, following roads
  to the ends of the earth,
  pilgrims on your way
  to the end of the age.

●● You are travellers on the road
  to freedom, a community
  of grace, with good news
  for all you meet.

- Travel lightly, travel together,
  learn as you go; you are
  disciples, the mission is urgent,
  the journey is long.

●● Travel with authority,
  be fearful of no one;
  you are apostles, opponents
  of evil, heralds of hope.

- Travel with humility,
  no task is too menial; you
  are servants, the cross is your
  compass, love is your sign.

●● Take heart; when the way
  is uncertain, shadows are sinister
  and dangers threaten, do not
  be afraid, I will be with you.

  Lord, you have promised
  always to be our guide.

I will never leave you
nor forsake you.

You are risen.

And I am still with you.

*You were with us
at the beginning.*

I will be with you
at the end.

Thanks be to God.

Now and for ever.

Amen.

2

Call and commission

You are an exodus people, familiar with deserts,
delivered from bondage for the freedom of others,
wayfarers following roads to the ends of the earth,
pilgrims on your way to the end of the age.

Terry Falla

For other prayers and readings with
this theme, see those entitled:

The call of freedom has been
   sounded 21
Called to serve the cause of right 23
Mercy and freedom are his gifts . 26
To make your purpose our
   purpose 35
Maker of heaven and earth 37
There is a new world 43

Risen and still with you 52
The goad of the promised future . 66
But not alone 147
Between already and not yet ... 170
The new commandment 251
The commitment of the
   community 298

Our call and commission

● Eternal God,
Maker of the universe and the atom,
Creator of màn and Lord of history,
we take your name upon our lips
and offer you our praise
at your invitation.

In our searching for you,
we discovered it was you who found us.
You have made yourself known to us
as the God and Father of our Lord Jesus Christ.

You have called us to follow him,
and you have commissioned us
as his disciples to a double-edged task:
to make your love known and live the Good News,
resist wrong and oppose evil.

Lord, we have often tried to tell you
that for such a task we are inadequate,
ill-equipped and unprepared.

Yet you always overrule our objections
and won't give in to our protests.
You recommission us
with the promise of your grace,
and the reassurance of your presence.

As we look back through the years
and forward to the future,
we therefore ask you to remind us
of the many dangers and fears,
difficulties and frustrations
we have encountered in the past;

That you never promised to protect us from trials,
or remove obstacles from our path;
to lift the burden of decision from us,
or the responsibilities of discipleship.

To the contrary,
it is to the way of the cross
that your Son, the carpenter of Nazareth,
has called us.

●● But remind us also
of the food we found in the wilderness,
of sin that has been forgiven,
of healing for wounds which seemed incurable,
of hope that has been restored.

God our Father,
we need reminding,
because our memories are short:

We forget that there is a hand that holds us,
a heart that thinks of our good;
we forget that you throw bridges across
the chasms we fear and consider impassable.

Lord, we need you to sweep
the dust from our minds
and the cobwebs from our hearts:

When in the face of adversity
we have said,
'We can't go on',
you have replied,
'I will be with you'.

When in times of depression and doubt
we have said,
'We have failed, we are defeated',
we heard you saying,
'Do not be afraid, for I am your God.
It is I — not your doubt or anxiety —
you must allow to be master of your life.'

- Most gracious God,
  let this also be true for our future.
  When in our travels together,
  or on a path we must tread alone,
  we are once again brought to a halt
  by danger, difficulty, or disaster:

  When the storms of disappointment rage,
  we see goodness crucified
  and the forces of evil advance,
  the cost of discipleship is all too clear,
  and we long to retreat to the comfort of clichés,

  Encounter us with your Son Jesus,
  that he may reawaken our understanding of you;
  tell us again who we are,
  and to whom we really belong.

  Lord, if this much we know, then we will have
  courage to endure and strength to continue;
  we will have tomorrows filled with promise,
  a joy to be shared, and Good News to proclaim.

The community of grace

Our Father, we thank you
that in our work and our worship
your Son Jesus *has* been in our midst;
that your Holy Spirit *has* moved among us,
shaken our complacency, questioned our orthodoxy,
and challenged our conformity.

We confess there are many ways
in which we have failed to change,
ways in which selfishness still wins,
and divisions remain.

There are ways
in which our need for security
and longings for recognition
make us measure our lives
by the standard of the crowd,

Our achievements
by the size of our salary,
the location of our street,
the impressiveness of our house,
or the make of our car.

Nevertheless, you have summoned us
to adapt ourselves no longer
to the pattern of this world,
but to rise above the narrow confines
of race and culture, creed and colour.

You have brought us together to be a new creation,
a community marked by love, and we thank you
for the ways in which this is true.

But never let us forget your words to us,
'I have chosen you to be with me',*
and that being with you does not mean
belonging to a closed or exclusive circle,

Quotation is from Mark 3:14 TEV

61

but rather following you into the world
to be your disciples irrespective of the consequences.

Lord, keep us aware that we can be the servant church
only as long as we allow you
to transform our lives.

Let our worship be an encounter with you,
and lead us to more awareness of each other,
our studies to new ways of expressing our faith,
our participation in your church and world
to relationships that last and allow others
to know you as their Lord.

And let our care for each other increase
until in reality it becomes the task
and concern of the whole church,

So that in hardship there is sharing,
in sickness there is support,
in grief there is comfort,
and in loneliness there is friendship.

Our Father, on this first day of the week
we praise you that it is by your grace we
are called, and by your mercy we are sustained,
so that we can follow you into the world
and be the church by sharing
in your death and resurrection.
Amen.

Our mission in the world

- Eternal God, when we respond to your call,
  you sweep us into that movement
  which takes the Good News
  to the ends of the earth.

  You have commissioned us to be the people of God
  in every nation and area of life:
  in local issues and international affairs,
  in the suburb and the ghetto,
  the city and the outback.

  You leave us in no doubt that to be your disciples
  we must travel lightly and be wayfarers on the road,
  that we need the Bible in one hand,
  and a newspaper in the other,
  a map of the world and
  a local street directory.

  Today we therefore pray for the mission of the
  church universal and the efforts of each
  local church community: for the work
  of your kingdom here in Australia
  and in every part of our planet.

- And, as we pray for a greater awareness of the world,
  and a deeper understanding of your purpose for it,
  we ask that you will take from us
  any hint of the hypocrisy which is willing
  to support those who are afar,
  while failing to recognize or refusing to acknowledge
  the needs and concerns of our own country.

  We pray for the men, women, and children
  who have come to our shores as refugees
  in search of a new home and a new life.

We remember also our Aboriginal brothers and sisters
who lament more than two hundred years of
hatred and opposition, prejudice and poverty.

O Father of the crucified Christ, at this time
give to these your people throughout this continent
as they fight to regain rights that have been negated,
and lands of which they have been dispossessed:

Faith amidst the ashes of disillusionment,
dignity to resist the forces of discrimination,
and courage to face the uncertainties of the future.

Lord of our nation,
as Australians we must share in dismay
at what has been done in our name;

We have allowed those with authority and power
to define the problems and the solutions,
forgetting that people are at stake.

Touch the heart of our nation, O God,
and give it a new integrity;
may justice once again roll down like a river
and righteousness like an ever-flowing stream.

- But no less, O Lord,
  do we pray for our own district,
  and ask that in it we may incarnate your presence.

Lord of all nations,
if in our own work for your kingdom
we have been apathetic in our affluence
or indifferent in our attitudes;

If we have lacked the strength to love,
have let cynicism blur our vision,
or bitterness cripple our soul,

In your mercy forgive us,
stir us again into action,
and inspire us to new endeavours.

Make us imaginative in our proclamation,
impatient with all injustice,
and unselfish in our support of others.

And now may your love,
the grace of our Lord Jesus Christ,
and the fellowship of your Holy Spirit,
be with us and remain with us always.

For yours is the kingdom, the power,
and the glory, for ever and ever.

Amen.

The goad of the promised future

We are a pilgrim people
on a journey which has no end
this side of history.

● 'Those who hope in Christ can no longer put up with
reality as it is but, beginning to suffer under it,
move to contradict it. Peace with God means
conflict in the world because the goad of
the promised future stabs into the flesh
of every unfulfilled present.'*

●● Lord Jesus Christ, we thank you that, when in the pages
of history your people have sought your presence,
you have indeed been with them to comfort and goad,
encourage and guide; and we praise you
for all the ways, all the moments, and all the years
in which this has been true for ourselves.

Always you have called us to be the servant church,
restless with the yearnings of your Spirit.

You bid us not to dwell on days gone by,
nor to thrust the ways of the past into the future.

Rather, reconciling us to yourself, you have given us
the work of handing on this reconciliation:

To suffer with your suffering in the world,
and rejoice with your rejoicing in the world.

Carpenter of Nazareth, crucified and risen, accept our
praise, hear our prayer, and help us fulfil our calling.

Thus, Lord Jesus, with the hope you have set before us,
may our whole life, and the life of this church
community, be shaped by the compassion of
the loving, suffering, redeeming God.

*Jürgen Moltmann

Praise and thanksgiving

Prayer in its initial, spontaneous form
of thanksgiving is the joyful ability
to accept the primal goodness of God.

Kornelis Miskotte

For other prayers and readings of
praise and thanksgiving, see those
entitled:

Summons to praise	21	God gives	134
Praise him, all creation	22	Against the wind	156
Gloria in excelsis	40	Mary's song	201
Life can begin again	46	The unexpected at every turn	233
God's everlasting kindness	50	The wind of the Spirit	283
The goad of the promised future	66	Fortitude	326
Sharing	134	Step into joy	338
Many lovely things	134		

Alive!

Alive!
We thank you, Lord,
whose finger touched our dust,
who gave us breath.

We thank you, Lord,
who gave us sight and sense
to see the flowers,
to hear the wind,
to feel the waters in our hand,

To sleep with the night
and wake with the sun,
to stand upon this earth,
to hear your voice,
to sing your praise.

Our hearts are stirred
with each new sight and sound.

Like a stream
the whole world pours into our lives,
and eyes, and hands,

And fills our souls
with the joy of gratitude
and living gladness.

We want to embrace
and experience and express
every good thing in your world.

O Lord our God,
how excellent is your name.

We do not take an untravelled way

- Eternal God,
  we praise you for this world, our home,
  and for every sign of your presence within it.

  Today we especially thank you
  for our church community,
  that to us it is a sign of your presence.

  We thank you, our Father,
  for those who had the vision
  to establish it,
  for those who had the audacity
  to believe you could use it.

  We acknowledge that at no time
  has the task been an easy one —
  and, while we seek to serve you,
  never will be.

  For this reason we praise you
  for every person whose perseverance
  has brought us to this day.

  For every person who has given
  mind, skill, and money.

  For every person who has devoted
  energy, time, and imagination.

  Most of all, our God,
  we thank you that, in spite of
  our failures, disappointments, and loss,
  you have been among us,
  disturbed us with your presence,
  and encountered us with your Son.

•• We thank you, Lord, for the present
in which we live and work:

*That in it we experience
your forgiveness, mercy, and love;*

That from it we can look back, reflect,
and with a deeper understanding of ourselves and you,
be better prepared for the road before us;

*And that, for sharing its pain and pleasure,
its sorrow and joy,
you have given us each other.*

We thank you, our Father,
for those persons in our church
with whom we share a special relationship:

*For those who are an example and inspiration to us,
for those who encourage us,
and give new strength for the journey,*

For those who show us patience and understanding,
for those who accept us as we are,
and love us without demand.

*For such persons, Lord,
we are more grateful than we can tell.*

• We praise you also, our Father, for the future,
which you are opening out before us,
and where you surprise us with the unexpected.

*We thank you that it belongs to you,
so that, come what may, we are met by your grace
and can journey in hope;*

That we are not asked to take an untravelled way
or choose our direction blindfold:
you have set the crucified Christ before us
as risen Lord,
and promised that we can share his life.

Most gracious God, we praise you
that you have given us a beginning,
and will be with us at the end;
that in the strength of your love we
can follow you to the edge of time
and the threshold of eternity.
For yours is the kingdom,
the power, and the glory,
for ever and ever. Amen.

Joy comes in the morning Psalm 30: selections

I will praise you, Lord,
for you have lifted me
out of the depths,
and not let my enemies
gloat over me.

O Lord my God,
I called to you for help,
and you have healed me.

O Lord, you have brought me
up from the grave,
and saved me from sinking
into the abyss.

Sing to the Lord,
you who love him;
remember his holiness,
and praise him.

His anger lasts only a moment,
his favour lasts a lifetime;
tears may linger at nightfall,
but joy comes in the morning.

Your love is strong enough

Eternal God,
we lift up our hearts and praise you
for the unlimited power of your love in Jesus Christ.

We thank you, we praise you,
because he never stopped loving you
even when his disciples ran away
and death stared him in the face;

Because he never stopped loving other people
even when he was being nailed to the cross;

Because the worst that men could do
in sending Jesus out to die
could not stand in the way of your love;

Because you showed us the power of your love
in raising him from death;

Because by his dying and rising again
we know that your love is strong enough
to go on loving till the end of time.

Lord, we praise you because we know
your love must win in the end.

Amen.

Patience that waits our returning

We give thanks to you,
God our Father,
for mercy that reaches out,
for patience that waits our returning,
and for your love that is ever ready
to welcome sinners.

We praise you
that in Jesus Christ
you came to us with forgiveness,
and that, by your Holy Spirit,
you move us to repent
and receive your love.

Though we are sinners,
you are faithful and worthy
of all praise.

We praise you,
great God,
in Jesus Christ our Lord.

Amen.

Thanks for our heritage

Lord God,
we thank you for those
who have given us
our immediate heritage:

Those from whom we learnt
to speak and walk,
to read and write,
to think and understand,

To know beauty
and to see goodness,
to learn of the world,
and to recognize you.

There are those who have
put up with us and carried us,
covered up for us and forgiven us,
believed in us and even enjoyed us.

There are those who have
forced us to work for our own good,
imposed some order and justice
into a muddled life,
encouraged us when we were despairing.

There are those who have
laughed with us and not at us,
protected us with their understanding
when we were under fire from others.

There are those whom
we have taken for granted.

There are those who have
allowed us to take advantage of them.

And there are those who
love us, and accept us as we are.

Lord, accept our thanks for every person
who has helped to shape
what we have become and are becoming,
in the name of Jesus.
Amen.

Recognizing the bonds

Our Father God, we thank you for teaching us
how to save each other and ourselves,
to give and to receive,
and to support each other on life's journey.

There is no limit to our ascent,
for there is no limit to the goodness we can do.

There is no joy we cannot have,
for there is no end to giving.

There is no height we cannot attain,
for we are created to need each other's
love and understanding.

The doors of the kingdom are open to all mankind,
so let us share our blessings and enter in.

In the past week we may have denied
happiness to others and to ourselves,
for selfishness lies in the way;
we are often enemies to our own happiness.

But through your Son Jesus, our brother,
you call us back to the truth.

We learn again the way to change hatred
into love, and to banish bitterness.

We know again the strength for good that is in
our grasp, and see your image shining in us.

Blessed are you, Lord, who teaches us to serve each other,
and to proclaim your goodness and mercy to all people.

Fun times

Thank you, God, for sunny days,
for my favourite colours,
and dogs with wagging tails.

*Thank you, God, for trees to climb,
and cubbies to hide in,
for parks with slides and swings.*

Thank you, God, for my gum boots
and my rain coat, for puddles
to splash in, and leaves to kick.

*Thank you, God, for beach balls
and surf boards, for warm sand
and the cool sea to swim in.*

Thank you, God, for friends to play with,
and for everyone who loves me very much.
Thank you, God, for me.

Amen.

Of driving clouds and open skies

O God, we thank you for this universe,
our great home, for its vastness and its riches,
and for the diversity of the life
which teems upon it and of which we are part.

We praise you for the arching sky
and the blessed winds, for the driving
clouds and the constellations on high.

We praise you for the salt sea
and the running water, for the everlasting hills,
for the trees, and for the grass under our feet.

We thank you for our senses,
by which we can see the splendour of the morning,
hear the jubilant songs of love,
and smell the breath of the springtime.

Grant us, we pray you, a heart wide open
to all this joy and beauty, and save our souls
from being so steeped in care,
or so darkened by passion,
that we pass heedless and unseeing
when even the thornbush by the wayside
is aflame with the glory of God.

Amen.

Grass by the roadside

All good giving and every perfect gift comes from above,
from the Father of the lights of heaven.
With him there is no variation,
no play of passing shadows.

James 1:17

Thank you, Lord, thank you
for all the gifts you have given me today,
for all I have seen and heard and received.

Thank you for
the water that woke me up,
the soap that smells good,
the toothpaste that refreshes.

Thank you for
the clothes that protect me,
their colour and their style.

Thank you for
the food that sustained me,
the cool and welcome glass of water.

Thank you for
the car that took me where I wanted to be,
the fuel that made it go,
the company of a fellow traveller.

Thank you for
the trees that nodded to me on the way,
the wind that caressed my face,
the grass by the side of the road.

Thank you for the tranquil night.
Thank you for the stars.
Thank you for the silence.

Thank you for the time you have given me.
Thank you for life.
Thank you for grace.

Lord of the storm Psalm 29

Pay tribute to the Lord, you sons of the gods,
tribute to the Lord of glory and power,
tribute to the Lord for the glory of his name;
worship the Holy One when he appears.

The voice of the Lord resounds over the waters:
the glory of God thunders,
echoes over the mighty ocean.
The voice of the Lord in power!
The voice of the Lord in splendour!

The voice of the Lord shatters the cedars,
the voice of the Lord shatters the cedars of Lebanon,
making Lebanon leap like a calf,
Sirion like a young wild bull.

The voice of the Lord
sharpens the shafts of lightning!

The voice of the Lord sets the wilderness shaking,
the Lord shakes the wilderness of Kadesh.
The voice of the Lord makes the oaks to whirl,
it strips the forest bare.

In his palace everything cries, 'Glory!'
As the Lord ruled over the deep waters,
so does he rule as king for ever.

May the Lord give strength to his people.
May the Lord bless his people with peace.

The earth is yours

From depths of earth to mountain top
everything comes under his rule;
the sea belongs to him, he made it,
so does the land, he shaped this too.

Psalm 95:4,5

Mighty God, the earth is yours,
and nations are your people.

Take away our pride
and bring to mind your goodness,
so that, living together in this land,
we may enjoy your gifts and be thankful:

For mountains and river valleys,
fern glades, water rippling over stone,
bush, weary of winter, drenched
in golden wattle, creeks draped with
the spoils of flood and storm and time;

For sweeping beaches, thundering surf,
drift-wood, tide pools, seaweed awash,
spinifex sand-dunes combed by the wind,
inlets, coves, and quiet shores;

For rain forests, plains of grass,
oceans of ragged blue grey-green scrub,
deserts, listless, bewitching, treacherous,
flecked with fragile vagabond beauty;

For cities, suburbs, country towns,
farms and outback stations,
where people work to harvest and shape
those things we need for living.

Lord of the earth, we thank you
for this land of variety,
colour and contrast,
and for all who strive
to make it just and generous.

Lord of creation, we thank you for all
whose respect for our planet and its
peoples widens our vision, helps us do
your will and see your purpose hidden
in our nation's history. Amen.

In awe and welcome stand   Psalm 8

O Lord, our Lord,
how great your name throughout the earth.

Above the heavens is your majesty chanted,
by the mouths of children, babes in arms.
You set your stronghold firm against your foes
and subdue enemies and rebels.

I look up at your heavens, made by your fingers,
at the moon and stars you set in place —
what is man that you should spare a thought for him,
the son of man that you should care for him?

Yet you have made him little less than a god,
you have crowned him with glory and splendour,
made him lord over the works of your hands,
set all things under his feet,

Sheep and oxen, all these,
yes, wild animals, too,
birds in the air, fish in the sea
travelling the paths of the ocean.

O Lord, our Lord,
how great your name throughout the earth.

Cosmic hymn of praise   Psalm 148: selections

Let the heavens praise the Eternal:
Praise him in the heights,

Praise him, sun and moon,
praise him, shining stars!

Let them all praise the name of the Lord,
at whose command they were created.

Let earth praise the Lord:
sea-monsters and all the deeps,
fire and hail, snow and mist,
gales that obey his decree,

Mountains and hills
orchards and forests,
wild animals and farm animals,
creatures that creep, and birds on the wing,

All kings on earth and nations,
princes, all rulers in the world,
young men and girls,
old people and children, too!

Let us all praise the name of our God,
for only he is supreme.

Lament

To suffer in God's way means changing
for the better and leaves no regrets,
but to suffer as the world knows suffering
brings death.

Paul of Tarsus

For other prayers which may be used
as laments, see those entitled:

I have betrayed 98
Tensed against tenderness 110
Failed 114
Belonging 135
Find your love 154
The true wilderness 242
Forsaken? 269
Holiness 320

Out of the depths   Psalm 130

Out of the depths I call to you, O Lord;
Lord, hear my cry.
Let your ears be attentive
to the voice of my pleading.

If you, O Lord, should mark our guilt,
Lord, could anyone survive?
But with you there is forgiveness:
and for this we revere you.

I wait for the Lord with all my soul,
and in his word I put my hope.
My soul is longing for the Lord
more than a watchman
for the coming of dawn.

Then let us rely on the Lord
as much as the watchman on the dawn;
for with him there is love unfailing,
and great is his power to set us free;
it is he who redeems his people
from all their sins.

Broken bones may joy   Psalm 51: selections

Have mercy on me, O God, in your goodness,
in your great tenderness wipe away my faults;
wash me clean of my guilt,
purify me from my sin.

For I am well aware of my faults,
I have my sin constantly in mind,
having sinned against none other than you,
having done what you regard as wrong.

Instil some joy and gladness into me,
let the bones you have crushed rejoice again.
Hide your face from my sins,
wipe out all my guilt.

God, create a clean heart in me,
put into me a new and constant spirit,
do not banish me from your presence,
do not deprive me of your holy Spirit.

Be my saviour again, renew my joy,
keep my spirit steady and willing;
and I shall teach transgressors the way to you,
and to you the sinners will return.

Save me from death, God my saviour,
and my tongue will acclaim your righteousness;
Lord, open my lips,
and my mouth will speak out your praise.

Sacrifice gives you no pleasure;
were I to offer holocaust, you would not have it.
My sacrifice is this broken spirit;
you will not scorn this crushed and broken heart.

My days are in your hand

Almighty God,
great sorrow has come over me;
my cares would overpower me;
I know of no way out.

God, be gracious and help me;
give strength to bear what you have sent;
let me not be overcome by fear;
give fatherly care for my loved ones.

Merciful God, forgive my sins
against you and my fellow men.
I trust your grace, and give my life
entirely into your hands;

Do with me as it pleases you,
and as it is good for me.
Whether I live or die, I am with you
and you are with me, my God.

Lord, I look for your salvation
and your kingdom.

Amen.

Things that make me sad

Dear Father God, there are
many things that make me happy,

*But sometimes there are things
that make me sad.*

Sometimes I am sad
when something I like
gets broken or lost.

*I am sad when a pet
of ours dies, or when
a friend's pet dies.*

I feel sad when good friends
go away and I don't see them
for a long time.

*But most of all I am sad
and don't like it at all when someone
I know or love very much dies.*

I think of people who have lost
their father or their mother,
and of everyone who is sad.

*Even though they are sad now,
may they soon be happy again.*

Amen.

He is hidden

- Why, God? Why? Why, when our need
  is desperate, when all other help is vain,
  do you turn away from us?

- Why? Why, when the darkness is deepest
  and our midnight is starless,
  do you hide yourself from us?

- Why, in times of grief and distress,
  when there is no light in the window,
  do we find a door slammed in our face,
  and a sound of bolting and
  double bolting on the inside?

- Why forsake us when we need you most?
  Why are you present when the skies are clear,
  our help in our days of prosperity,
  but so absent in our time of trouble?

- Why, like your servant Job, do you give us
  reason to feel that 'Were he to pass me,
  I should not see him', like your prophet
  Jeremiah to feel deceived, angry, desolate?

- We know that faith does not exempt us from sorrow
  or shield us from evil — we know that; we know, too,
  that the earth is wet with the blood of the innocent —
  but why this? Why now? Why?

- Know this, God, know this: if faith were dependent
  on feelings, if our trust in you were no more than
  a matter of the mind, we would be done with you,
  done with you now, done with you for ever.

- And hear this, God, hear this: if it were not for
  that man who was friend of the poor and the damned,
  for that man who healed the sick
  and gave sight to the blind;

- If it were not for that man whom we cursed
  and crucified, and who is crucified still,
  for that man who bore our griefs and carried
  our sorrows, and who carries them still —

•• God, God eternal, God of Jesus, God who said
  'Yes' to his life, his love, his suffering, his death,
  God of the cross, crucified God, sharing our pain,
  bearing our sin, if it were not, O God, for you,
  for you our lover, you our judge, you our hope,
  you our friend, we would indeed be lost.

God of Christ,
God who raised him from the dead,
God with whom life can begin again,
come to us now, hold us, help us, heal us,
for you and you alone are our salvation.

Shafts of trust Psalm 13

How long, O Lord, will you forget me?
How long will you hide your face?
How long must I bear grief in my soul,
this sorrow in my heart day and night?
How long shall my enemy prevail?
Look at me, answer me, Lord my God!

Give light to my eyes lest I sleep in death,
lest my enemy say: 'I have overcome him';
lest my foes rejoice to see my fall.
But I trust in your unfailing love,
my heart rejoices in your saving help.
I will sing to the Lord
for the goodness he has shown me.

Longing for tomorrow and losing today

- Lord,
  I search
  for some sense
  in life.

  *I look
  for some tomorrow
  when I shall see —
  and know.*

  And then
  life will begin
  to have pattern
  and meaning.

  *But what I have
  is today.
  I see dimly,
  I know little,
  and life is very ordinary.*

  So I wait
  for tomorrow,
  dreamily, and
  allow my today
  to slip by.

  *Vague anticipation
  of fulfilment some day
  robs me
  of the only day
  that is truly mine.*

•• Lord, God,
you have called me
to live in the *now*;
air castles
aren't for real:
life is.

If this were
the only day
I had on earth,
what would I do
with it?

This *is*
the only day
I have right now;
I dare not
waste it.

Lord,
keep me keenly,
sharply aware
of the immediacy
of my living.
Keep me
vitally awake
this day.
Amen.

Rebellion

• Some days we find it hard to love you, Lord;
we smoulder with rebellion, even in church.

*Your way of managing this world seems wrong;
your love and justice appear to be missing.*

From the Middle East to Ireland, Argentina to Australia,
we confront a tangle of suffering.

*From Washington to Moscow, Canberra to Peking,
there is no clear path that leads to a better world.*

The world shudders with injustice and torture;
hatreds and fear spawn the agony of wars.

*All the efforts of nobler people bear poor fruit;
prophets, seers, and poets die unfulfilled.*

Well-meaning politicians are reduced to cynicism;
their ideals perish under the weight of 'respectable' corruption.

*Scientific discoveries are prostituted by pride, greed, and war;
even gifted physicians serve the rich rather than the sick.*

•• It seems your fault, Lord!
You made this world where tragedies occur!

*Why did you create the possibility of greed?
Or the neglect of your Aboriginal children?*

The neuroses that afflict high-rise living?
And the stupidity of poker machines and the road toll?

*You permitted the opening for graft and corruption;
you allow injustice and starvation to continue.*

In us you have placed a hunger for a better world,
but we lack the ability to build that world.

*None of us are able to put into practice all we believe;
you let us wander among our broken promises.*

Lord, to whom can we turn?
Where can we find adequate resources?

• Lord, if it were not for Jesus of Nazareth,
we would have given up long ago.

If his forgiveness and renewal were removed,
we would slip away into dark despair.

But because you have given us one proper man
in whom salvation takes glorious shape,

There is hope for us all,
there is joy at the end of the travail.

O let our lives become filled with his grace!
Weld our souls to the steel of his soul!

Transform our rebellion into renewed discipleship;
replace our anger with a fresh discipline.

Help us to see your love at work in darkest places,
and to recognize your glory in tiny victories.

O lead us into the new creation begun in Jesus!
Raise up your new nation among all nations!

A people on trial Based on Micah 6:1-8

● Stand up and let the case begin
in the hearing of the mountains,
and let the hills hear what you say.
Listen, you mountains, to God's accusation,
give ear, you foundations of the earth,
for God is accusing his people,
pleading against the church.

●● My people,
what have I done to you,
how have I been a burden to you?
Answer me.

I rescued you from the dominion of darkness,
and brought you away to the kingdom of my dear Son.
For you there is a new world: the old order has gone,
and a new order has already begun.
From the days of Luke the physician and Paul of Tarsus
I have sent apostles and prophets to you;
you know of their deeds and have their writings.

My people,
have you forgotten,
can you no longer recall:

The broken bread, the cup, the Mount of Olives,
the act of Pilate when he washed his hands,
the complicity of the crowd and the call to crucify?
The gibbet and a world plunged in darkness:
curses, desolation, fear; helplessness, death, despair?
The grave and resurrection morning:
disbelief, awe, joy; hope, freedom, faith?

With what gift shall we come before the Lord,
and bow down before God on high?
Must we come with promises of perfection,
with assurances that we will keep every rule,
strive always to be very good?

••• What is it that the Lord asks of us?
What answer can we give him?
What worship shall we offer him?

Will he be pleased with church every Sunday,
with a life spent seeking to gain his favour?
Must we spurn every happiness
for the wrong we have done,
live all our days in denial and gloom
to atone for our sin?

• This is what the Lord requires,
this is what he seeks and longs for,
only this:

That you live to the full
the life that he gives —

Hear that Jesus our Lord was delivered to death
for our misdeeds, and raised to life to justify us;

Believe the good news that by faith we have been
put right with God and are at peace with him;

Accept his grace and his goodness
with open hands and open hearts;

Know that it is not sacrifice he desires,
but justice, mercy, and good faith;

And act upon the word of Jesus as he says to you,
'If you want to be a follower of mine,
leave self behind, take up your cross,
and come with me'.

Quotations have been taken from
Colossians 1:13
Romans 4:25; 5:1
Matthew 9:13; 23:23
The final stanza is based on
Mark 8:34

Eternal God and mortal man   Paraphrase of Psalm 90

O God, you have always been God.
Long before the earth was formed,
long after it ceases to exist,
you have been and you shall always be.

With you there is no beginning or end;
time is not measured by
decades or centuries.

Our lives, so important to us,
are but fleeting
shadows to you.

And they are so full
of trouble and conflict,
so marked by sin and failure.

O God, break into
our short span of existence
with your eternal love and grace.

May our days of despair
be interspersed
with hours of joy.

Enable us to see something
of your will and purpose
for our creation,
and to discover some meaning
for our brief and trouble-fraught
appearance in this world.

Imprint upon us
your brand of ownership,
and place us within
your plan and objective
for our lives.
Amen.

Confession and forgiveness

He knows too that henceforth he will never be afraid
of any power on earth, for once in his life he
faced life as a whole, and came to terms with it.
Once in his life, he really and completely
confessed his sins.

Hans Lilje

For other prayers and readings of
confession and forgiveness, see those
entitled:

Because you believe in us 32
Granting of forgiveness 177
You are accepted 228
The cost of discipleship 241
Temptation 244
Doing the truth 248
Forgiveness.................... 250
Shadows of fear................ 253
The darkness is never so distant 254

Confessions at the empty tomb . 272
Healings from the empty tomb . 274
The open church 288
A taste of sawdust and a thirst
  for truth 314
Gossip 317
Holiness 320
Transformed nonconformist.... 322

A plea for God's forgiveness   Micah 7:18-20

What god can compare with you:
taking fault away,
pardoning crime,
not cherishing anger for ever
but delighting in showing mercy?

Once more have pity on us,
tread down our faults.

Throw all our sins
to the bottom of the sea.

Grant us your faithfulness
and your mercy,
as you swore to our fathers
from the days of long ago.

I have betrayed

Lord, I have betrayed you
by following my own way.

I have denied you
by fearing to follow yours.

And I have mocked you
by not taking your death seriously.

Lord, I am lost.
Let your forgiveness find me.

Hold me in your strong arms
and give me your new life.

Live in me and with me day by day,
that together we may make a world
that is new.

If I flew to the point of sunrise Psalm 139: selections

Lord, you examine me and know me,
you know if I am standing or sitting.
You read my thoughts from far away;
whether I walk or lie down, you are watching,
you know every detail of my conduct.

The word is not even on my tongue, Lord,
before you know all about it;
close behind and close in front you fence me round,
shielding me with your right hand.
Such knowledge is beyond my understanding,
a height to which my mind cannot attain.

Where could I go to escape your Spirit?
Where could I flee from your presence?
If I climb to the heavens you are there;
there, too, if I lie in Sheol.

If I flew to the point of sunrise,
or westward across the sea,
your hand would still be guiding me,
your right hand holding me.

It was you who created my inmost self,
and put me together in my mother's womb;
for all these mysteries I thank you:
for the wonder of myself, for the wonder of your works.

You know me through and through,
from having watched my bones take shape
when I was being formed in secret,
knitted together in the limbo of the womb.

God, how hard it is to grasp your thoughts!
How impossible to count them!
I could no more count them than I could the sand;
and, suppose I could, you would still be with me.

God, examine me and know my heart,
probe me and know my thoughts;
make sure I do not follow pernicious ways,
and guide me in the way that is everlasting.

Jesus

He was careless about himself,
we are careful.

He was courageous,
we are cautious.

He trusted the unworthy,
we trust those who have good collateral.

He forgave the unforgivable,
we forgive those who do not really hurt us.

He was righteous and laughed at respectability
we are respectable and smile at righteousness.

He was meek,
we are ambitious.

He saved others,
we save ourselves as much as we can.

He had no place to lay his head
and did not worry about it,
*we fret when we cannot have
the last convenience manufactured by clever science.*

He did what he believed to be right
regardless of consequences,
*we determine what is right
by how it will affect us.*

He feared God
but not the world,
*we fear public opinion
more than we fear the judgment of God.*

He risked everything for his Father, God,
we make religion a refuge from every risk.

He took up the cross,
*we neither take it up
nor lay it down
but merely let it stand.*

Father, forgive,
and, in the freedom of your forgiveness,
*may we climb to the threshold of our belief in you,
take up our cross and follow your Son.*

Amen.

You shall know the truth and the truth shall set you free   John 8:32

- In this question of truthfulness,
  what matters first and last
  is that a man's whole condition
  should be exposed, his whole
  evil laid bare in the sight of God.

•• But sinful men do not like
  this sort of truthfulness,
  and they resist it
  with all their might.

- That is why they persecute it
  and crucify it.

  *It is only because we follow Jesus
  that we can be genuinely truthful,
  for then he reveals to us
  our sin upon the cross.*

•• The cross is God's truth about us,
  and therefore it is the only power
  which can make us truthful.

  *When we know the cross,
  we are no longer
  afraid of the truth.*

Beyond all pretence

We confess to you, Lord,
what we are:
we are not the people
we like others to think we are;
we are afraid to admit even to ourselves
what lies in the depths of our souls.
But we do not want to hide
our true selves from you.
We believe that you know us as we are,
and yet you love us.
Help us not to shrink
from self-knowledge;
teach us to respect ourselves
for your sake;
give us the courage to put our trust
in your guiding and power.

We also confess to you, Lord,
the unrest of the world,
to which we contribute
and in which we share.
Forgive our reliance
on weapons of terror,
our cold indifference
to the needs of others,
our discrimination
against people of different race,
our preoccupation
with material standards.
Forgive our being unsure
of the good news about you and from you,
and so unready to tell it,
share it, and live it.

Raise us out of the paralysis of guilt
into the freedom and energy
of forgiven people.
And for those who through long habit
find forgiveness hard to accept,
we ask you to break their bondage
and set them free.
Through Jesus Christ our Lord.
Amen.

Put your name upon us

- We are grateful for God's free gifts and for
  his grace touching the lives of so many. Seeing
  our own limited witness, in sorrow and shame we
  turn to him, acknowledging our sin and asking
  him to make us new in Christ.

●● O Lord our God, we have failed to do your will:
  we have lived in fear of ourselves
  and refused to be free in Christ.

*Forgive us for our lack of confidence in you,
our lack of hope in your reign,
our lack of faith in your presence.*

Others have lived in chains
and we have not cared enough;
we have shut out the voices
that plead for justice.

*Forgive your church its wealth among the poor,
its fear among the unjust,
its cowardice among the oppressed.*

We have not died to selfishness
in order to live for others:
we have gone our own way and found no peace;
we have lost ourselves and forsaken our name.

*Put your name upon us,
restore us to your covenant with your people.*

Turn our evil will and uphold us when we are weak,
ban us from the empty word,
bring us to true repentance.

*Teach us to honour your will
for the love of Jesus Christ,*

Make us strong with the vitality
of your Holy Spirit.

For you alone are our Saviour and our God.

Father, forgive

The hatred which divides
nation from nation, race
from race, class from class:

Father, forgive.

The covetous desires of
men and nations to possess
what is not their own:

Father, forgive.

The greed which exploits
the labours of men and lays
waste the earth:

Father, forgive.

Our envy of the welfare and
happiness of others:

Father, forgive.

Our indifference to the plight
of the homeless and the refugee:

Father, forgive.

The lust which uses for
ignoble ends the bodies of
men and women:

Father, forgive.

The pride which leads us to
trust in ourselves and not in
God:

Father, forgive.

We give you what we are

From the unsteady heights of our own goodness
and importance, we sometimes look down
on the frailty of others.

O God, we offer you this ignoble pride;
replace it with humility.

At other times we feel that we are nothing,
that most other people are more successful,
capable or effective than we are.

O God, we offer you our feelings of inferiority;
make us realistic and honest in our
estimation of ourselves.

Sometimes our professions are high,
but our practice is low.
We are not always the people
we make ourselves out to be.

O God, we offer you our hypocrisy;
help us to be open and sincere.

There is much more that could be confessed:
personal and public sins, individual and corporate
sins, sins of commission and omission, conscious
sins and sins of ours of which we are not aware.
It is not our acts of confession and contrition
which maintain us as God's people; it is the
mercy and grace of God upon which
we are entirely dependent.

O God, we offer ourselves to you;
we give you only what we are.
The taint of sin touches us.
But we also feel the redeeming touch
of your more abundant grace.
Amen.

Free to forget our pride

Father,
we ask forgiveness
for everything that is wrong in our lives.

If we are jealous of somebody,
or resentful and bitter about anything;

If we have hurt or offended others
or treated other people unfairly;

If we have gone back on our word
or forgotten to keep our promises;

If we have been dishonest or deceitful
or conspired against someone for our own advantage:

In the name of Jesus Christ,
Father, forgive us and help us.

Help us to see and admit all our faults
and make amends where we can.

May we be so secure in the knowledge
of your forgiveness and love
that we may become free
to forget our pride,
let go of resentment,
and be at peace with you,
with other people,
and with ourselves.

Through Jesus Christ our Lord.

Amen.

The times we talk too much

Dear Lord,
we come confessing.

There are times
when we talk too much.

There are times
when we repeat things
which we have no right to repeat.

We pass on a story
which may not be entirely true,
or add our own embroidered flourish
to a tale in the telling.

Father, forgive.
This is a sin of commission —
and a dreadful betrayal of confidence.

Forgive, and help us to keep
a deliberate and constant
check on our tongues.

Keep safe within us
the hurts and secrets
that others have shared
with us as a trust.

Keep safe within us
the confidences and communications
which were entrusted to us
for safekeeping.
Amen.

Power

Eternal God,
you are the power behind all things:

Behind the energy of the atom,
behind the heat of a million suns.

Eternal God,
you are the power behind all minds:

Behind the ability to think and reason,
behind all understanding of the truth.

Eternal God,
you are the power behind the cross of Christ:

Behind the weakness, the torture, and the death,
behind unconquerable love.

Eternal Power,
we worship and adore you.

Father,
source of all power:

We confess that we do not always use the
powers you have given us as you intend.

Sometimes we are afraid of the power we
wield, and so do not use it at all:

At other times we are careless in our use
of it, and harm others.

At yet other times we deliberately misuse it
to achieve our own selfish ends:

We confess our misuse of our God-given powers,
and ask for your wisdom and grace to use them
properly in the future.

Amen.

Tensed against tenderness

• We have been called by God to be the Church,
the Body of Christ in his world.
We are not a building,
but vibrating, pulsating people,
grounded in the Word of God,
the love of Christ,
and the fellowship of the Holy Spirit.
Let us acknowledge
how far short we have fallen.

Lord, hear our prayer,
and let our cry come unto you.

Our Father, you come to us
with gracious and gentle touch,
to reveal and remove the sins
and the faithless practices
which hold us down,
spoil our effectiveness,
and destroy our wholeness of spirit.
Grant us, therefore,
the gift of real repentance,
that we may also know
the beauty of your 'shalom':
your peace.

Lord, hear our prayer,
and let our cry come unto you.

Our Father, you bid us to love one another
and become an open supportive community,
mature and able enough
to offer succour to those around us.
But we confess that we are often defensive,
unable to bear any criticism,
whether it be constructive or otherwise,
and we are unable to speak honestly
lest we hurt feelings,
and upset the equilibrium.

We confess with sorrow how shallow
and fragile our relationships often are,
so that we have grown insensitive to the way
your Spirit moves to make men whole.

Lord, hear our prayer,
and let our cry come unto you.

Christ, we are tired of being your Body
in name more than in reality —
talking big, using Bible words,
but acting small and making you unbelievable.
We are tired of being shallow,
hard, tight, tensed against tenderness,
guarded against becoming involved in real caring,
afraid to follow new winds of your Spirit.
We want to move out of our insensitivity.

•• Lord, hear our prayer,
and help us admit our self-centredness.

Forgive us, and set us free
from narrow and selfish standards,
remind us that the Son of Man
came not to be served, but to serve;
teach us to forgive
and let go of old resentments,
to care even in the face
of hostility and rejection,
to love each other and your world
as you have loved us.

Lord, hear our prayers,
and help us admit our smallness of spirit,
narrowness of mind, and hardness of heart.

Lord, forgive us;
furnish us with the courage
to seek fresh guidance from your Word,
and then to be open and responsive to your Spirit,
as you seek to comfort and reprove us,
disturb and lead us. Amen.

Blindness   John 9:39-41

Eternal God our Father, forgive us
when we deplore violence in our cities
if we live in suburbs where lawns
are clipped and churches enlarged;

When we condemn the apathy of our society,
if we have closed our eyes to our own
comforts and affluence.

Forgive us for cheering legislators
who promise low taxes, but deny homes
and schools to those in need;

For self-righteousness that blames
the poor for their poverty
or the oppressed for their oppression.

Forgive us for not wanting to recognize our
relatives in your family who are black or red
or yellow or white, whose children's children
may be our grandchildren;

For accepting people we like,
but rejecting those we do not like,
because they are not of our class or colour.

Forgive us for turning our churches into
private clubs, for loving familiar hymns and
religious feelings more than we love you;

For pasting stained-glass on our eyes and our
ears to shut out the cry of the hungry and
the hurt of the world.

Forgive us for bypassing political duties,
for condemning civil disobedience
when we will not obey you;

For reducing your holy law to average virtues,
by trying to be no better or worse than most men.

Participants in evil

Almighty God,
our heavenly Father,
we have sinned against you
and against our neighbours near and far,
in thought and word and deed;

*In the evil we have done
and in the good we have not done,*

Through ignorance, through weakness,
through our own deliberate fault.

*We are truly sorry
and repent of all our sins.*

For the sake of your Son,
Jesus Christ our Lord,
who died for us,
forgive us all that is past;

*And grant that we may serve you
in newness of life
to the glory of your name.
Amen.*

Failed

Almighty God,
whom we call Father
because of the obedience
and sacrifice of Jesus-Messiah,
we come before you in silence,
for we have failed:

*Failed to be the imprint of your image,
failed to be your stewards
before people and over nature,
failed to reflect your love and mercy,
failed to be servants of reconciliation.*

And yet, Father, we pray to you
because we long to be trustworthy,
showing the impact of your love
in our lives, acting out justice
as you will it.

*Therefore, O God, do not take
your Spirit from us, but implant
in us the image of your Son.*

Justify us *with* him
and lead us through this world
toward your kingdom.

Amen.

Penitence

Lord God Almighty,
forgive your church:

Its wealth among the poor,
its fear among the unjust,
its cowardice among the oppressed.

Forgive us, your children:

Our lack of confidence in you,
our lack of hope in your reign,
our lack of faith in your presence,
our lack of trust in your mercy.

Restore us to your covenant
with your people.

Bring us to true repentance.

Teach us to accept
the sacrifice of Christ.

Make us strong with the comfort
of your Holy Spirit.

Break us where we are strong.

Make us where we are weak.

Shame us where we trust ourselves.

Name us where we have lost ourselves:

Through Jesus Christ our Lord.
Amen.

Take fire

Lord God,
take fire and burn up
our guilt and hypocrisy.

Take water and wash away
our brother's blood
which we have shed.

Take warm sunshine and dry
the tears of those we have hurt,
and heal their wounded souls,
minds, and bodies.

Take love and plant it in our hearts,
so that brotherhood grows,
transforming the dry deserts
of our prejudice and hatred.

Take our imperfect prayers and make them pure,
so that we mean what we pray,
and are prepared to give ourselves
to you, through Jesus Christ,
our Lord. Amen.

Intercession

For it is one thing to see the land of peace
from a wooded ridge . . . and another
to tread the road that leads to it.

Augustine

For other prayers of intercession, see
the sections Call and Commission,
and Commitment, in Part Two, and
the prayers and meditations entitled:

Our utmost need 27
Where your treasure is 155
Against the wind 156
The rhythm of community 158
The pledge of the Spirit 193
The insatiable desire 202
Light of the world 226
A surprising start 230
Where the Spirit of the Lord is,
   there is freedom 236
Choices 240
Vision and mirage 246
Doing the truth 248
The darkness is never so distant 254

When little is left 256
The threshold 257
Who takes away the sin
   of the world 260
Breath of our life 279
Lord of the winds and fires
   of earth 280
In the stillness 281
Powers beyond our own 282
The open church 288
Transformed nonconformist 322
Fortitude 326
Step into joy 338

A prayer of Ignatius Loyola

Teach us, good Lord,

To serve you as you deserve;
to give and not to count the cost;
to fight and not to heed the wounds;
to toil and not to seek for rest;
to labour and not to ask for any reward
save that of knowing that we do your will:
through Jesus Christ our Lord.

Amen.

Ignatius Loyola:
c. 1491-1556

Steps marking our way

Lord, you are our God.

*We want to realize how much
we depend upon you.*

You have not only given us life;
you have made us able to think about its meaning
and to choose and work for what is good.

*In the world much is confusing;
many voices strive to be heard.*

Yet we have your Word to guide us,
the life and teaching of your Son,
the example of many faithful Christians.

*We have known your hand holding us fast,
your steps marking out the way for us;
we long to know you still.*

Your presence transforms even the darker times;
with you we need not be afraid,
for nothing can separate us from your love.

*Draw out from us such an answering love
that in our time of testing we may not fall away.*

Enough! John 1:18

Transcendent and eternal God,
how in our finitude, how in our humanity,
can we even pretend to know very much about you,
you, God of all creation, God of all ages,
God of all history, from everlasting to everlasting?

*But we praise you that we know enough —
enough because you have come to us in Jesus,*

Because of his birth in Bethlehem, not in Jerusalem,
his childhood in Nazareth, not in Rome,
his healing of the sick, his teaching of the kingdom,

*Because Jesus is the Good News,
the Good News about you and from you,*

Because of the people who followed him and were his friends,
the disreputable and the poor with whom he was identified,
his trial as a criminal, his execution as an outcast,

*Because your love cannot be killed
and no tomb can contain you.*

God of Jesus,
when reason fails and hope lies dormant,
break into our wilderness with the news
that because of him we know enough:
enough for our trust to be restored,
enough for our faith to be renewed,
enough to hold because we are held.

*Enough to know that you are our Father —
and that you will never let us go.*

Amen.

That dreams may be dreamt

Almighty God and merciful Father,
pour out on your church
the Spirit of your Son Jesus
so that dreams may be dreamt
and visions seen.

Open our eyes for his work among people,
so that we may join all those
who with persistence and humility
pursue his will for our world.

Holy Spirit of God,
who brooded over the waters
long before we were born;

Who inspired the people of God
to praise and trust;

Who lit the fire of the prophets
and sustained their faith
among unbelief;

Who fulfilled through our brother Jesus
the hope of the generations,
and revealed the dimensions of God;

Holy Spirit of God,
fill us with confidence
and make us available;

Teach us to pray
and to hear the cries
of God's children;

Help us interpret
the signs of the times;

And prepare us
for the kindgom of God
each day and for ever.
Amen.

The divine discontent

Our Father, Creator of heaven and earth,
who has so made us that to whatever heights we climb
we see yet loftier heights before us,
and, for ever being dissatisfied with our attainments,
perceiving that we ought to be outreaching what we are:
strengthen us in this divine discontent.

We lift up our hearts unto you, O Lord.

Free us, O God, from all manner of self-complacency,
from too much pride in the actual, and forgetfulness
of the ideal, and from contentment with the levels
on which our lives are lived.

We lift up our hearts unto you, O Lord.

We confess our temptation to measure our lives
by the standards of the crowd.
Grant us such clarity of vision,
independence of mind, and courage of will,
that we may live according to an enlightened conscience,
without fear or favour of the multitude.

We lift up our hearts unto you, O Lord.

Give us fresh visions of the possibilities
latent within us, and since what we are
is but the seed of what we may become,
grant to us the inspiration of your Holy Spirit,
that our hopes may become realities.

Lord, have mercy upon us, and grant us this blessing.

O God, who, without our seeking,
has set us in this world, give us light
that we may know the pathways we should tread.
Confirm in us the dreams of seers
and the hopes of prophets.
Let not cynicism blight, nor faithlessness uproot,
our confidence in your coming kingdom
of righteousness upon the earth;
and at the fire of our faith let courage be kindled
that we may live more nearly as we pray.

Lord, have mercy upon us, and grant us this blessing.
Amen.

The promise of your presence

All goodness and truth are yours, O Lord.
May no evil estrange us from you,
nor error darken our vision
of your purpose.

Help us to discern your justice
and to understand your will.

In adversity and prosperity,
let the promise of your presence
put strength into our souls.

Help us so to trust you
that we may not be afraid,
but may work with you
in the service of the world,
proving your love by our own,
through Jesus Christ our Lord.
Amen.

In all things be our strength

Eternal God, our Father, it is our prayer that
in all things you will be our strength, so that:

We may accept the responsibility of our freedom,
the burden of our privilege, and so conduct
ourselves as to set an example for those
who will follow after;

We may not be content with a secondhand faith,
worshipping words rather than the Word;

We may find joy in the study of Scripture,
and growth in exposure to new insights;

We may be part of our community, sharing in the
great mission you have set before us, and
always seeking the common good;

We may find in your church a prod to our
imaginations, a shock to laziness, and a
source of power to do your will.

O God, who gave us minds to know you, hearts
to love you, and voices to sing your praise:

Send your Spirit among us, that, confronted
by your truth, we may be free to worship you
as we should.

Through Jesus Christ our Lord.

Amen.

A letter not written with ink

Our Father, God,
as you confront us with your Word
and meet us in the world,
may we discover
and keep rediscovering:

*That 'true peace
is not merely the absence of tension,
but the presence of justice and brotherhood',*

That 'the ultimate tragedy
is not the brutality of the bad people,
but the silence of the good people',

*That 'with your help and the world's,
we can speak, share, and show forth
a substitute for selfishness and silence',*

That, as your people, we are
an open letter about Jesus Christ:

*'A letter written not with ink
but with the Spirit of the living God,*

Written not on stone tablets
but on the pages of the human heart'.

The first three quotations are
from Martin Luther King,
and the fourth from
Paul of Tarsus (2 Corinthians 3:3)

To know God is to do justice Jeremiah 22:16

That you will forgive our preoccupation with belief
rather than action, our involvement in the greed,
compromise, and hardness of our world, our distrust
of those who talk with a strange accent, or dress
in unusual clothes:

We ask you to hear us, O Lord.

That you will teach us to recognize the cries of those
who are too weak to help themselves, make us more
sensitive to the problems and fears which lie at
our door, and strengthen us to face with courage
and determination whatever loss, inconvenience,
or misunderstanding is needed to put things right:

We ask you to hear us, O Lord.

That you will rescue our worship this day from trivial
issues, narrow horizons, and superficial concerns,
and cast down the false gods we have fashioned through
prejudice, self-interest, fear, or wishful thinking:

We ask you to hear us, O Lord.

That you will increase in us spontaneity, friendliness,
and insight, so that in times of personal perplexity
and difficulty we may still as a community provide
the focus for true wisdom, genuine understanding,
and quiet optimism:

We ask you to hear us, O Lord.

That you will strengthen us to do battle against
unfair housing, unequal educational opportunities,
and narrow sectarian loyalties, and enable us to be
appreciative of the things we take for granted,
perceptive toward the things we ignore, and fair
toward the things against which we rebel:

We ask you to hear us, O Lord. Amen.

The Word was made flesh, he lived among us John 1:14

Lord Jesus Christ,
Word of Life,
we see full humanity only in you:
the image of what life can become.

*Your presence you make known to us
in the Church, your Body, and in the
joy and sorrows of our fellow humans.*

Lord Jesus Christ,
Prince of Peace,
you have brought together,
by your reconciling death,
'Jew and Greek,
male and female,
slave and free'. *

*So, from bondage set us free:
the bondage we inflict on ourselves,
the bondage we inflict on others.*

And save us from war,
from the death of the spirit,
from all hatred,
and from self-righteousness.

*Holy Spirit of God,
Living Fire,
give to us again your threefold gifts:
your gifts of faith, hope, and love.*

Give us faith in God,
hope in his future,
and love for all people.

*Through Jesus Christ our Lord.
Amen.*

* Galatians 3:28

God saw all that he had made, and indeed it was very good Genesis 1:31

Eternal God, our Father,
to all of us you have given
the mystery of life.

In Jesus Christ your Son
you have shared with us
your very self.

Help us, therefore,
to share our life
with others,
to give freely
from what you
have given to us.

You have blessed the earth
with rain,
with fruit,
with crops;

And we have your promise:
'As long as earth lasts,
sowing and reaping,
cold and heat,
summer and winter,
day and night
shall cease no more'. *

So grant us joy
in your goodness to us;
gratitude for this land
of sunshine and harvests.

* Genesis 8:22

We confess we have
misused your gifts;
we have spoilt
your creation.

*Too often
we are thoughtless,
or selfish
in our handling
of life's good things.*

So grant us
the grace of forgiveness
for the past;
the grace of responsibility
for the future.

*Through Jesus Christ our Lord.
Amen.*

Every part of our life

- Our Father God, we worship you
  as the one who has given us this life,
  and ask that you will help us
  to live it to the full.

  At home,
  may we be the fathers and mothers,
  sons and daughters,
  brothers and sisters,
  that we really want to be,
  so that our family
  may be a truly happy one.

  *Help us to spread the warmth of our
  home life to everyone we encounter.*

•• At school,
  may we be teachers and students
  who are stirred by
  the challenge of learning
  and excited by the joy of discovery.

  *Help us to develop the discipline
  that true adventure requires.*

- At work,
  may we be reliable,
  honest in what we do,
  and friendly to those
  who find things hard.

  *Help us always to give our best,
  to be workers who need not be ashamed.*

•• In our games,
  help us to play hard,
  but to play fair.

  *Help us to win without boasting,
  and to lose without making excuses.*

- In our pleasures,
  help us never to find delight
  where there is hurt
  for others or ourselves.

  Help us not to choose things
  we would rather hide,
  or some day bitterly regret.

●● Lord, may we be strong in character,
  loving in our relationships,
  forgiving when others fail us,
  and loyal.

  May our lives be useful to others
  and fulfilling for ourselves.

- We ask that in every part of our life
  you will help us
  to widen our knowledge,
  deepen our love,
  and strengthen our service.

  Through Jesus Christ our Lord.

  Amen.

Courage to change

Eternal God, our Father,
may your Spirit speak to us
in such a way
that we live out our lives
with the conviction that
'all that is necessary
for the forces of evil
to win in the world
is for enough good men
to do nothing'.

'Lord, give us:

*The serenity to accept
what cannot be changed;*

The courage to change
what ought to be changed;

*And the wisdom to distinguish
the one from the other.'*

Quotations are from
Edmund Burke and
Reinhold Niebuhr.

Limb and mind in harmony

Our Father, we thank you for giving us
and all your creatures a love of play.

Thank you for the pleasures
of eye and limb and mind
working in harmony, and for the
healthy environment we enjoy.

Help us to learn
from submitting to rules,
from belonging to a team,
and from accepting an umpire's verdict,
that self-discipline is worthwhile.

May the experience
of learning the skills of our sport,
of engaging in fair competition,
and of working to keep fit,
teach us the value of developing
all your gifts.

Help us to enjoy our victories
without losing respect for our opponents;
when we lose, make us generous toward them
and keen to improve ourselves.

Help us, with honest effort,
to fulfil our potential,
and to encourage our opponents
to do the same.

Keep us fair in judgment,
clean in play,
disciplined in mind and body,
as befits followers
of the Lord Jesus Christ.

Amen.

And please save us from ever saying
  'I never touched him, Ump!'

Sharing

God shares food and water,
God shares toys, beds, and tables,
God shares rooms and clothes,
God shares birthdays and balloons.

Many lovely things

I like to play on soft green grass,
I like to see the clear bright stars,
I like to see the water fall and hear birds that call,
I like the flowers and trees, the buzz of bees.

God gives

God provides our food and drink for the day,
he provides us with friends with whom we can play.
he has given me a family where I am happy to live.
Thank you, God, for looking after me.

Belonging

Dear Father God,
not everyone can run and jump,
can see, or hear and speak.

Not everyone has enough to eat,
or has a home to live in,
or parents to look after them.

We know that we are all different;
but sometimes we feel angry or sad
when we can't do or have
the same things as other people.

Help us all to make our church a family
where we can be different —
and yet know that we belong to it,

Where we can be ourselves,
and know that we love each other
— very much.

Amen.

Make us healthy-minded

Dear Father, help us
to make mistakes courageously
this week.

We know we cannot possibly hit
the mark in everything we try,
so let us try and keep trying.

Let us not weep when we fail
to fulfil our hopes and intentions,
but help us to keep striving.

May we be understanding
with the mistakes of others.

Help us to be a community marked by
caring and comforting,
healing and sustaining,
enabling and reconciling,
so that together
we may demonstrate our love
for you, for each other,
and for all people.

Thank you, Father, for the ability
to learn from mistakes, and to hone
our minds, skills, and spirits
so that the supreme goal,
even Christ, may be closer
through the efforts,
the mistakes, and the successes,
of this week. Amen.

Go with us, Lord

Father,
as we go to our homes and our work
this coming week,
we ask you to send the Holy Spirit
into our lives.

Open our ears:
to hear what you are saying to us
in the things that happen to us
and in the people we meet.

Open our eyes:
to see the needs
of people around us.

Open our hands:
to do our work well,
to help when help is needed.

Open our lips:
to tell others the Good News of Jesus
and bring comfort, happiness, and
laughter to other people.

Open our minds:
to discover new truth
about you and the world.

Open our hearts:
to love you and our fellow men
as you have loved us in Jesus.

Forbid!

Eternal Father, Creator of every planet and star,
of the wind and the seas and the rain,
give us today, we pray, the mind and heart
to rejoice in your creation.

*Forbid that we should walk through your beautiful
world with unseeing eyes.*

Forbid that the lure and comforts of technology
should ever entirely steal our hearts away from
the love of open acres and the green trees.

*Forbid that under the low roof of house or workshop,
office or study, we should ever forget
your great overarching sky.*

Forbid that when all your creatures are greeting
the morning with songs and shouts of joy,
we alone should wear a dull and sullen face.

*Let the energy and vigour which you have infused
into every living thing stir within our being.
May your life and joy pulse through us.*

And, above all, give us grace to use these beauties
of earth without us, and this eager stirring of
life within us, as a means by which we respond
to you, our Creator and our God.

Love which leads to awareness

No wonder then so many die of grief,
so many are so lonely as they die.
W.H. Auden

Lord God, the story of your love makes us realize
that there are many others as well as ourselves
who need your help and your grace;
so we bring our prayers to you:

For those who suffer pain,
and for those whose loneliness is soul-destroying;

For those whose minds are disturbed,
and for those who live lives of quiet despair;

For those who have not had the opportunities
to realize their potentialities;

For those who are satisfied with something less
than the life for which they were made;

For those who know their guilt, their shallowness,
their need, but who do not know of Jesus

For those who know that they must shortly die;
for those who cannot wait to die.

Lord God, your Son has taken all our sufferings
upon himself and has transformed them.

Help us, who offer these prayers, to take the
sufferings of others upon ourselves, and so,
by your grace, become the agents of your
transforming love:

Through Jesus Christ our Lord.
Amen.

For our city and ourselves

Hear us, O Lord, as we pray for our city.
Its beauty and its business
both lay hold upon us,
and we pray for it
as those who know
its squeeze upon ourselves
and upon our people,
and who take to heart the needs
that exist behind its steady, beating life.

Grant that fences
that keep potential friends apart
may be fashioned into bridges,
so that the hurts of any
may be the concern of all.

Help us to look for you,
and to find you, in the life we live
and the work we do.

If we take a drive
up into the distant ranges,
you are there.
If we tram our way
into the milling crowds
of our city's main street,
you are there.

If we ride the lift
to the topmost floor
of our tallest building,
even there shall your hand lead us
and your right hand hold us.

If in the dead of night
we feel deserted and depressed,
the darkness cannot hide us from you,
for all times and places
are your habitation.

You are our God, and we are your people;
so hear us, O Lord,
as we pray for ourselves.

Save us from being overworked
but unemployed.
Save us from spending time
without using life.
Save us from being authoritative
without being authentic.

We are so varied in our needs
that no one prayer can say it all.

Some of us are in a hurry,
and we find ourselves on a train
that stops at every station and signal.

Some of us are reeling
from a recent loss or relocation,
and what was rock beneath our feet
has turned to sand.

Some of us are suffering
from flagging self-esteem,
for those who knew us in our prime,
and remembered, keep moving on.

Some of us are caught up
in implementing change
that troubles us
because we are not sure
of all its implications.

O God, help us to know you as our Father,
and humble us to receive your grace.

Make us glad that we can never go
where you are not,

That we can never sink beneath
the level of your love. Amen.

A litany for the Lucky Country

For those whose dreams of freedom and equality
inspired our nation:

We give thanks, O God.

For those whose sacrifice and courage preserved
this country in times of danger and indifference:

We give thanks, O God.

For all who quietly yet firmly resisted wrong
without bitterness or vengeance:

We give thanks, O God.

For leaders who have placed righteousness and justice
before concern for prestige and popularity:

We give thanks, O God.

For the multitude of citizens whose hope and
deeds of mercy are known only to you:

We give thanks, O God.

From good intentions gone astray in this country
and across the earth:

O Lord, deliver us.

From the irresponsible use of natural resources,
of economic and political power:

O Lord, deliver us.

From a narrow patriotism which ignores the needs
and welfare of all people:

O Lord, deliver us.

From a preoccupation with the past and a refusal
to confront the future with faith and vision:

O Lord, deliver us.

From false pride and blindness to our nation's
frailty, from complacency and timidness
in speaking the truth:

O Lord, deliver us.

That the Prime Minister of our country and all
executive officers, legislators, and justices
may govern courageously, justly, and wisely:

Lord, send forth your Spirit.

That the people of this land may dwell together
in unity without fear:

Lord, send forth your Spirit.

That we may proclaim good news to the poor, release
to the captives, recovery of sight to the blind,
and liberty to all who are oppressed:

Lord, send forth your Spirit.

That the kingdoms of this world may be taken up
into the reign of your eternal kingdom:

Lord, send forth your Spirit.

A world in which faith comes hard

Lord,
we pray for this modern world
in which faith comes hard,
where people find it difficult
to raise their eyes
above the material things
which are so necessary to life.

We pray for those
who find it hard to believe
because they have too many things,
and for those who find it hard
because they haven't enough.

We pray for those
who have more to eat than they need,
and those who are dying from lack of food.

We pray for parents
who, because of their poverty,
and a lack of concern on the part of others,
must watch their children die.

We pray for those
who suffer from disease, from confusion
and guilt, from depression and fear.

We pray for those
who face each day with dread,
because their lives are so dominated
by the power of others.

We pray for those
who are so lonely that life is robbed
of all loveliness and hope.

Lord, we pray because our love for you
is a love for One whose compassion
embraces all human suffering.

We pray because you are in our midst,
and have made people in their need
present to us, and us aware of them.

We pray because you call us as
your disciples to reach out from ourselves
to all our fellow human beings.

Amen.

When in prison you came to my cell
Matthew 25:31-46

Our Father and our God,
opponent of all evil
and friend of the oppressed,

Inspire us with your love.

That there are people who hunger for warm rice,
or milk, or meat, or cheese,
or even the scraps our pets ignore:

Lord, help us to remember.

That there are people who hunger for your grace,
and search their minds and hearts for words of prayer,
who, having your love, yet fail to find its presence:

Lord, help us to remember.

That there are people who hunger to be free,
to go where they please, or stay upon their land,
or even to think, to laugh, to plan, to hope:

Lord, help us to remember.

That there are people who thirst to know the truth,
and have at hand some small, dry cup of lies
provided by cynical, evil leaders:

Lord, help us to remember.

That there are people who thirst to use themselves
and give of all they have learnt from life, but are
held back by the jealousy of their contemporaries:

Lord, help us to remember.

That there are people who thirst to create love
in loveless circumstance of slum,
or homeless circumstance of compound:

Lord, help us to remember.

That there are people naked to weather,
helpless before torture,
sick with disease and with loneliness:

Lord, help us to remember.

That there are people prisoner to the walls of tyrants,
and prisoner to the walls of indifference —
that in the least of these your kingdom awaits our love:

Lord, help us to remember.

Grant to us, O God, a total stewardship of self,
possessions, and endeavour,
by hour and by day, by moment and by night,
for the sake of him who came among us
to serve us all.

*Lord, keep us in the faith which sustains
all sorts and conditions of people.*

Amen.

But not alone

The old order is passing away; your new order, Lord,
has already begun, and we are numbered among its signs.
Through your Spirit in our hearts, you have set us free
and taught us to call you Father.

You have called us out of darkness
into your marvellous light.

You have opened our eyes, given us hope that we shall live
in the glorious liberty of the children of God.
But not alone, Lord; not while others remain poor,
broken-hearted, imprisoned, blind, and bruised. Yet —

You have called us out of darkness
into your marvellous light.

So, Lord, we pray for our brothers and sisters, your family,
oppressed by ignorance and poverty, caught in a web
of injustice and apathy, cut off from one another
by language, culture, colour, class, and creed.

You have called them out of darkness
into your marvellous light.

Through education may the powerless be led to self-discovery,
the despised find new dignity, the dispossessed be enabled
to claim their place in the community of free people.

You have called them out of darkness
into your marvellous light.

Give to your church a vision of the total liberation
of humanity. Grant us the wisdom to hear the voice
of the foolish of the world, and strength to listen
to the weak, that through those who are nothing
we may understand the word of Christ.

You are calling us out of darkness
into your marvellous light.

But we tend to love darkness rather than light.
We shrink from the responsibility of freedom,
the uncertainty of the desert, the conflict of the cross.
We keep turning back, preferring the security
of slavery to the adventure of the promised land.

Call us out of darkness
into your marvellous light.

Call us, Lord Jesus Christ, that we may follow —
follow you not only as the one who goes ahead,
but as one who journeys with us, freeing us, uniting us.

And let us, O Lord, be content to learn
the meaning of your way as we walk in it.

Amen.

The unquenchable hope

Eternal God, we believe that our worship
draws us to you
and toward our neighbours on earth.

We pray for the whole creation:

May we all learn before it is too late
to respect the uniqueness, fragility, and beauty
of our earth and all its creatures.

We pray for every nation and race:

May our actions and lifestyle bear out our belief
that all people everywhere are our brothers and sisters,
whatever their country, their city, or their tribe,
whatever their education or their culture,
whatever their circumstances, religion, or colour.

We pray for peace in our torn and troubled world:

We pray that weapons may be discarded instead of people,
guns silenced instead of the voices of the poor,
and that, in a world half-expecting nuclear holocaust,
we might learn that love is not a luxury.

We pray for the church in every part of our globe:

May it be true and joyful, wholesome and active,
always rediscovering that you called it into being
for the service and salvation of others.

We pray for the witness of our local church community:

As we grow in faith, and hope, help us to understand
that no planning for the future, however necessary,
no program, no matter how carefully conceived,
can relieve us of the necessity of going forward
into a future that cannot be planned —
of risk, of danger, of hope
in your incalculable grace.

We pray for ourselves:

Not one of us has ever found or given enough love
in his or her life, enough truth, freedom,
beauty, goodness, and joy.
We are always living for a new 'tomorrow'.

Lord, we pray for our world, we pray for others,
we pray for ourselves.

We pray because you have put within us
an unquenchable hope.

We pray because we live for the ultimate.
We pray because Jesus is our Lord
and your kingdom is in our midst.

Amen.

Peace prayer of Francis of Assisi

Lord, make me an instrument of your peace.
Where there is hatred, let me sow love,
where there is injury, pardon,
where there is doubt, faith,
where there is despair, hope,
where there is sadness, joy.

O Divine Master,
grant that I may not so much
seek to be consoled as to console,
to be understood as to understand,
to be loved as to love.

For it is in giving that we receive,
it is in pardoning that we are pardoned,
it is in dying that we are born again
to eternal life.

Offering

No one gives himself freely and willingly to God's
service unless, having tested his Father's love,
he is drawn to love and worship him in return.

John Calvin

For other prayers especially suitable
for the offering, see those entitled:

Your word and your truth in
  our midst 25
To make your purpose our
  purpose 35
The community of grace 61
Our mission in the world 63
Recognizing the bonds 75
Fun times...................... 76
Grass by the roadside 78
The earth is yours 80
Put your name upon us 104
A prayer of Ignatius Loyola 118
That dreams may be dreamt ... 121
God saw all that he had made.. 128
Sharing........................ 134

God gives 134
A world in which faith
  comes hard 144
When in prison you came
  to my cell 145
Peace prayer of Francis of
  Assisi........................ 150
Venturing the harder road 164
Liberty to the oppressed........ 166
Redemptive suffering 168
Between already and not yet ... 170
The open church 288
The commitment of the
  community 298

With what gifts shall we come before him?

Isaiah 58

You seek me day after day,
you long to know my ways,
you ask me for laws that are just,
you long for me to draw near.

But is not this the worship that pleases me
— it is I the Lord who speaks:
to break unjust fetters
and let the oppressed go free?

Is it not sharing your food with the hungry
and bringing the homeless into your home,
clothing the destitute when you meet them,
and not evading your duty to your own flesh and blood?

Then if you call, I will answer;
if you cry to me, I will say, 'Here I am'.

Yes, if you do away with the yoke of injustice,
the clenched fist, and the wicked word,
if you share what you have with the hungry,
and satisfy the needs of the wretched,

Then your light will rise like dawn out of darkness,
and the Lord will be your guide continually;
he will satisfy your needs in desert places,
and you will be like a spring whose waters never fail.

Whatsoever you do

When I was hungry, you gave me to eat,
when I was thirsty, you gave me to drink,

When I was homeless, you opened your doors,
when I was naked, you gave me your coat,

When I was weary, you helped me find rest,
when I was anxious, you calmed all my fears,

When I was little, you taught me to read,
when I was lonely, you gave me your love,

When in a prison, you came to my cell,
when on a sick bed, you cared for my needs,

In a strange country, you made me at home,
seeking employment, you found me a job,

Hurt in a battle, you bound up my wounds,
searching for kindness, you held out your hand,

When I was Black, or Chinese, or White,
mocked and insulted, you carried my cross,

When I was aged, you bothered to smile,
when I was restless, you listened and cared,

You saw me covered with spittle and blood,
you knew my features, though grimy with sweat,

When I was laughed at, you stood by my side,
when I was happy, you shared in my joy.

'I tell you, whenever you did this for one of
the least important of these brothers of mine,
you did it for me.'

A meditation
by Mother Teresa of Calcutta
based on Matthew 25:35-46

Find your love

Many people are out of touch —
out of touch with others,
out of touch with themselves.

Too busy to remember others exist,
never loving others,
unable to love themselves,
unable to love those hungry for love,
unable to love those lost and friendless.

People are dying for love.
Without love,
people are unable to live.

Those that don't know love need our love;
they want to be filled with love,
never to hunger again.

Where your treasure is, there will your heart be also

For all the sad words of tongue or pen
the saddest are these,
'It might have been'.

John Greenleaf Whittier

Save us, O Lord, from the sadness,
from the tragic and self-destroying sickness:

Of being so imprisoned by self-pity,
or trapped by the need for security,

So rigid with self-righteousness,
or ruled by self-imposed principles,

So embittered by disappointments,
or hardened by cynicism,

So blinded by self-deception,
or cornered by false pride,

So lured by success,
or tempted by prestige,

So seduced by possessions, subservient to money,
or captive to the myth that to have leads to happiness:

That we lose the passion for living and loving,
the courage for daring and hoping,

That we lose the freedom for growing and changing,
the capacity for giving and receiving,

The humility for learning,
the tenderness for understanding,

The strength for enduring,
the trust for believing —

And forfeit for ever
the joy of your kingdom.

Counterfeit?

Holy Father, we bring
this money to you.

*If it represents no sacrifice,
but merely a superstitious habit
or a tiresome formality,
then awaken us to our fault.*

If it represents an act of love
and a genuine sacrifice,
then keep us from pride,

*And increase our ability to give
even ourselves to your will.*

Amen.

Against the wind

• How easy it is for me to live with
    you, Lord!
How easy it is for me to believe in
    you!
When my thoughts get stuck or my mind
    collapses,
when the cleverest people see no further
    than this evening,
and do not know what must be done
    tomorrow,
you send down to me clear confidence that
    you exist,
and that you will ensure not all the ways
    of goodness are blocked.

From the summit of earthly fame I look round
   with wonder at the road through hopelessness
   to this point
from which even I have been able to shed abroad
   among men the reflection of your glory.
And you will grant me to express this as much
   as is necessary,
and, in so far as I am not able to do it, that
   means that you have allotted the task to others. *

•• Lord, as together we give for the work
and witness of your church in the world,
we thank you for every person whose life
gives perspective to our own.

We thank you for the man whose words
we have just heard, and for every person
whose quiet courage and regnant faith
stirs within us the pulse of new hope,
and enables us also to lean into the wind.

Lord, may the task you have allotted to us,
and what others do that we cannot,
be woven together into your design
for every people and all creation.

Amen.

* Alexander Solzhenitsyn
exiled Russian author ·

The rhythm of community

Lord, we come before you, not alone,
but in the company of one another.

We share our happiness with each other —
and it becomes greater.

We share our troubles with each other —
and they become smaller.

We share one another's griefs and burdens —
and their weight becomes possible to bear.

May we never be too mean to give,
nor too proud to receive.

For in giving and receiving
we learn to love and be loved;
we encounter the meaning of life,
the mystery of existence —

and discover you.

Never too poor to be generous

'Toiling, one must help the weak,
remembering the words of
the Lord Jesus, when he said,
"There is more happiness in giving
than in receiving".' *

*Almighty God, there is no doubt
about the adequacy of our receiving.*

Let there be no doubt about
the generosity of our giving.

*Accept our offering,
through Jesus Christ our Lord.*

Amen.

Using our gifts

God our Father, with these gifts
we offer you our lives
to do your work in the world.

Take our bodies and our minds,
our work and our leisure,

Our relationships with other people,
our friendships and our family life,

Our dreams and our doubts,
our faith and our plans for the future.

In the name of Jesus Christ our Lord,
we bring them to you.

Amen.

* Acts 20:35

Yours is the kingdom

Yours, Lord, is the greatness,
the power and the glory,
the victory and the majesty;

For all that is in the heavens
and in the earth is yours,
and you rule over all.

Therefore, Lord, receive these offerings,
our tangible expressions
of love and gratitude.

Touch them into life for many,
so that your kingdom may grow
in the hearts of men.

In the name of Jesus.

Amen.

We commit ourselves to live in love   Luke 10:27

'You must love the Lord your God
with all your heart,
with all your soul,
with all your strength,
with all your mind
and your neighbour as yourself.'

Our Father, God,
we make these offerings
as a pledge of our love and loyalty,
to you, to each other, and to all
our fellow human beings.

We commit ourselves to live in love,
and to be everybody's loyal servants,
in the name of Christ,
our Servant Lord.

Amen.

Messengers of hope

Eternal God, author of our life,
in your Son, Jesus Christ our Lord,
we find wholeness, see our true
identity, and discover the meaning
and purpose of our existence.

With gratitude and praise we offer
ourselves, with our talents and treasure,
to be messengers of your Good News:

To let people know
that you are with them,

To save them from despair
and to give them hope,

To save them from fear
and to give them confidence,

To save them from death
and to give them life.

In the name of Jesus Christ,
our living, reigning Lord.

Amen.

Bread with laughter

We offer to you, Lord, our money.

We offer to you, Lord, ourselves.

We offer to you the work of the world
in this neighbourhood and beyond.

*Grant that men and women may work
with joy and dignity.*

Grant that children may have
bread with laughter.

*And grant that we may reflect
in our work and in our lives
the community we have found
in the sharing of the loaf,
and the presence we have known
in the breaking of the bread.*

Amen.

Commitment

If anyone wants to be a follower of mine,
he must leave self behind; day after day he
must take up his cross, and come with me.

Jesus

For other prayers of commitment, see
those entitled:

Praise for the past and trust
  for the future 39
Our call and commission 58
The community of grace 61
Our mission in the world 63
The scandal of grace 178

The insatiable desire 202
To the end 258
The commitment of the
  community 298
Glimpses of a winding road 302
Fortitude 326

Venturing the harder road

To love someone else's life
more than our own,
to reach out in support
of another person's weakness
when we ourselves are falling,
to give another person hope
when we are close to despair,
and to offer forgiveness
when we are unforgiven;
this is what you ask of us, Lord,
and it is hard:

Hard to give
when we are poor;
hard to help
when we need help;
hard to encourage
when we are discouraged.

Yet Jesus loved
when he was hated;
he forgave
when he was crucified;
and he won eternal life
for all mankind
by his own death.

It is to faith in him
you call us —
not in ourselves;
we are not asked
to take an untravelled way
or to choose
our direction blindfold:

You have set
the crucified Christ before us
as risen Lord,
and promised
that we can share his life.

So, Lord,
with this assurance
we will make our decision
to love others
better than ourselves,
and to give them
life and hope
whatever the cost.

We will press on
knowing that you are with us,
leading us to fullness of life
which cannot be taken away.

Go with us, then,
into the troubled
and perplexed world,
in which we too will be
troubled and perplexed.

Go with us,
and help us
to calm trouble
and heal perplexity:

Carrying on our shoulders
the cross,
and in our hearts
the joy of service,
until Christ's work is complete
and you are glorified for ever.
Amen.

Liberty to the oppressed

- Let us pray now for people everywhere,
  for all entrapped in structures of injustice
  and all who struggle for liberation,
  for the leaders of the nations,
  and all who claim to be disciples of Christ.

•• Eternal God, we pray for people of every nation,
  developed or developing, affluent or poor:

  For those whose poverty is spiritual,
  and those whose poverty is material.

  For people who hunger for justice and freedom,
  and those whose hunger is for food.

  For people whose wealth is their poverty,
  and those whose poverty robs them of dignity.

- We pray that divisions in this one world may
  be healed, and peace more actively pursued,

  That justice may be achieved for the oppressed,
  fears and tensions eased, and exploitation brought to an end.

  We pray that those who shape policies may learn
  to balance conflicting claims more equitably,

  And that the apathy of the affluent may be
  transformed into compassion and care.

•• We pray for reforms in our economic system,
  that people may matter more than profits,

  That the disadvantaged may have the justice of fair prices,
  and that the powerful may refrain from using tariffs unfairly.

  We pray for those who work in and control the media,
  and who, by what they say and write, exert wide influence,

  That they may reverence truth, disarm prejudice,
  dispel ignorance, and sharpen discernment.

• We pray for those who are easily influenced
and aroused to hatred and partisan conflict,

*For those who too easily make peace with
the demands of social and political systems,*

For the young, that they may find all that makes for
a free spirit, and generous, courageous purpose,

*For those whose age is a barrier to action,
but whose wisdom can help to change the world.*

•• We pray for men and women in their daily lives:

For those who do too little and expect too much,

For those who earn too little and work too much,

For those who want to work and cannot.

• We pray for people who are alone and lonely,
and have no one to whom they can turn,

*For those who are in despair, finding
the burden of living too great to bear.*

We pray for people who suffer constant pain,
or struggle with traumas of the mind,

*And for those who give their time and energy,
understanding and sympathy, to others who are in need.*

•• We pray for all who know themselves to be called
to live under the lordship of Jesus Christ:

*For those who need encouragement and support
as they struggle against prejudice and injustice,*

For those whose faith in action
results in persecution or imprisonment,
and brings sorrow to them and their loved ones,

*For ourselves, that despite the cost
we will avoid false divisions
between personal and social aspects of salvation.*

• Lord, we offer this prayer as a pledge of our love and loyalty, to you, to each other, and to all our fellow human beings.

With the gift of your Spirit, we commit ourselves
to live in love, to bear your cross in our world,
serving it with compassion, imagination, and courage.

In the name of our Saviour,
Jesus Christ our Lord, we pray.

Amen.

Redemptive suffering

Lord Jesus Christ,
your suffering and death
are the source of our hope and joy.

In you the mighty love of God
faced the worst the human race can do,
yet in the cold darkness of death
we see the fire of love,
and recognize the depth of his mercy.

We realize that the world
is as cruel now
as it was then.

Despair and death still swallow up
our hopes and our triumphs,
and the evil in all our hearts
still crucifies goodness.

As we pray for the world,
we remember how profoundly you cared,
and we realize
that we cannot stand aside, uncaring:

We cannot stand aside while
men and women suffer and die,
while they go hungry
and are deprived of justice and love.

And, remembering your sorrow,
we know that we cannot hide
from the sorrow of others,
or run away from the things
which cause sorrow to ourselves.

Lord Jesus, we ask for ourselves
and all who are your disciples,
that, where men and women are in despair,
in anxiety, or in loneliness,
we may share your suffering
and proclaim the love and mercy of God.

Until in us your sorrows
have run their course,
and love's final work is finished.

Cause us to remember, Lord,
that you have chosen us
and commissioned us:
to pray and to work,
to live and to die
for the human race.

Lord, for the world's sake
keep us faithful to you,
so that we may always put
love before ambition,
and goodness before success,
to the honour of your name.

Amen.

Between already and not yet

Our Father God, you call us to be a community of change,
to act with you in transforming the world into
the community of our Lord and Saviour Jesus Christ.

*Through his life and death you have shown us
that to accomplish our mission you require us
to live in the world but not of it;*

That we cannot escape from the world *and* be
faithful; yet, neither can we be so enmeshed
in the world that we lose our souls.

*We confess, Lord, that we find your call to live
simultaneously in this world and in your community,
to live all the time on the border and always risk
disagreement and error, to be difficult and demanding.*

Nevertheless, in the strength of your love,
renewed by your grace, and confronted by your
Word, we commit ourselves to you as a people
to whom you have given a peculiar memory —

*A memory of being called continuously to leave
where we are, and to go somewhere else and be
someone else, a people never staying still
or holding on to present understandings and ways.*

We commit ourselves to you as a people
to whom you have given a peculiar vision —
a vision of a world not yet realized
and yet already come;

*A people from whom you demand dissatisfaction with life
as it is, whom you haunt with the promise of a new age,
and pull toward its fulfilment.*

We commit ourselves to you as a community
to whom you have given a peculiar hope —
a hope that gives meaning to life
as a pilgrim people on a mission under
the power and purpose of the Gospel;

*A hope that proclaims that persons and institutions
can change, that people and public orders can be
transformed to embody more fully your will for
justice, freedom, harmony, community, and peace.*

We come in worship to praise you for your mercy
which is more than our minds can measure, to confess
that we have wavered in our loyalty to you, and to
celebrate the presence of the risen Christ in our midst.

*We come and we ask in the name of Jesus our Saviour
that you will judge our sin, shatter our complacency,
speak to our fears, strengthen our resolve, and then
send us into your world to discern and do your will.*

Amen.

Our ultimate loyalty

As with our brethren here we meet,
thy grace alone can feed us.
As here we gather at thy feet
we pray that thou wilt heed us.
The power is thine, O Lord divine,
the kingdom and the rule are thine.
May Jesus Christ still lead us!*

Lord God,
may there be sense in our persistence,
and reason in our tenacity.

May our existence as your people
not be deemed an end in itself,
but solely a way and a means.

May we live our lives conscious of our past
and true to our heritage, keeping ablaze
the fires our prophets lit.

May we, like our fathers
still stand out against the multitude,
protesting with all our might
against its follies and its fears.

May a divine discontent
give colour to our dreams,
and a passion for holy heresy
set the tone of our thoughts.

May the soul of the rebel
still throb in us as it throbbed
in our forefathers, that, refusing
to be silenced, we may take the part
of those without a voice.

* From the Anabaptist *Ausbund*, 16th century,
translated by E.A. Payne

And may our ultimate loyalty
be only to you, that we may never
surrender to the threat of falsehood,
or capitulate to the idols, caesars,
and powers of this world.

Thus, with the hope you have given us
in your Son, Jesus Christ our Lord,
may we follow him today and for ever,
that we may proclaim without fear or favour
the Gospel of your suffering, redeeming love.
Amen.

Come, Lord Matthew 10:34

Come, Lord.

Do not smile and say
you are already with us.

Millions do not know you;
and to us who do,
what is the difference?

What is the point of your presence
if our lives do not alter?

Change our lives,
shatter our complacency.

Make your Word
flesh of our flesh,
blood of our blood,
and our life's purpose.

Take away the quietness
of a clear conscience.

Press us uncomfortably.

For only thus
that other peace is made:
— your peace.

Celebration

Then they told their story of what
had happened on the road,
and how they had recognized him
at the breaking of the bread.

The Gospel of Luke

The following prayers are intended for use before the breaking of the bread and the sharing of the cup:
Granting of forgiveness
The scandal of grace
Given for the life of the world
Just as we are
We are your family
Do this, remembering me
Brought together to break bread
The thanksgiving
Sounds of the Sacrament

'We share his peace' may be used before or after the Lord's Supper.

The following prayers are intended for use after the breaking of the bread and the sharing of the cup:
You have met us in your Son
The pledge of the Spirit
Dreams for celebration

The two last named may also be used in many other contexts.

Granting of forgiveness 1 John 1:8-10

If anyone sins, we have someone
who pleads with the Father
on our behalf —
Jesus Christ, the righteous one.
And Christ himself is the means
by which our sins are forgiven —
and not our sins only,
but the sins of the whole world.

Most merciful God,
we confess that we have sinned against you
in thought, word, and deed.
We have not loved you with our whole heart.
We have not loved our neighbours as ourselves.
We pray that you will have mercy upon us,
*   that you will forgive us*
*   for what we have been,*
*   that you will help us*
*   to amend what we are,*
*   that you will direct*
*   what we shall be;*
that we may delight in your will
and walk in your ways,
through Jesus Christ our Lord. Amen.

God wills that all people should be saved,
and in response to his call
we have acknowledged our sins;
he pardons those who humbly repent
and truly believe the Gospel.
Therefore we have peace with God,
through Jesus Christ,
to whom be blessing and honour for ever.

Amen.

The scandal of grace

The offence of Easter was Jesus'
accursed death on the cross —
his table-fellowship with sinners
was the pre-Easter scandal.

Joachim Jeremias

Lord Jesus Christ, as we break this bread
and put this cup to our lips, we would remember
that we are in unusual company:

The company of every disciple, every outcast,
every hesitant follower, with whom you
broke bread, drank wine, and shared a meal;

The company of every person who knew
in your presence the grace of God
and the joy of the kingdom;

The company of the poor, the sick, the blind
and the lame, with whom you laughed,
with whom you wept, and whom you healed;

The company of beggars, prostitutes, and
extortioners, the demented and the insane,
the disillusioned and the condemned;

Of Mary from Magdala, sneered at, avoided,
the subject of whispers, haunted by shadows
of a demon-dark past, to whom you gave
womanhood, dignity, freedom, and life;

The company of Zacchaeus and Levi,
self-seeking, unscrupulous, hated, unhappy,
to whose homes you were welcomed,
whose lives were transformed;

Of Simon the zealot, disciplined, dedicated,
insurrection in his thoughts, revolution in his dreams,
impatient for the overthrow of his people's oppressors;

The company of Thomas, doggedly loyal,
determined, unyielding, wanting the truth,
but unwilling to settle for a second-hand faith;

Of Peter the fisherman, once bold, then broken,
alone with the memory of a friendship betrayed,
whose love you affirmed in the dawn by the sea.

With the breaking of bread and the fruit
of the vine, you offered them peace and friendship,
trust and forgiveness, the love of the Father,
the fellowship of God.

Lord Jesus, with the church through the ages
we join them today; we share their need,
we have their doubts, we know their failures,
we too are sinners hungry for grace.

We come in their company, hesitant, eager,
scarcely daring to believe this incredible news,
this offence to propriety, the scandal of your love,
for them, for the world — for us.

With awe, with amazement, in worship,
we break the bread, we share the cup,
we hear your words, 'Until I come',
we confess you, Lord, now and for ever.
Amen.

Given for the life of the world

The bread that I shall give
is my flesh,
for the life of the world.
John 6:51

We do not presume
to come to your table, merciful Lord,
trusting in our own righteousness,
but in your manifold and great mercies.

We are not worthy of your goodness and grace,
but you are the same Lord
whose nature is always to have mercy.

Grant us, therefore, gracious Lord,
so to eat the flesh of your dear Son Jesus Christ,
and to drink his blood,
that we may evermore dwell in him,
and he in us.

Amen.

We are your family

Lord Jesus Christ,
we thank you for inviting each one of us
to be part of this church family.

Help us never to think of our position in it
as one of privilege, but as an opportunity
to serve each other and your world.

Help us as members of one family
to be constantly aware of the needs
of the rest of the family,
and keep us humble.

Lord, help us never to make trouble,
but always to work for peace,
to be open, warm, and honest,
motivated always by your love.

Help us never to stand on the letter
of the law, never to be concerned with
our own rights, our own place,
our own importance.

*As we come together to receive
your bread and cup, make us
bread ready to be broken,
wine ready to be shared,
to meet the needs of all your children,
and be your presence in the world.*

Amen.

Just as we are

● Merciful God,
our hands are unclean,
our hearts are unprepared.

*We are not deserving
of your love and acceptance.*

But your love, beyond all comprehension,
compels us to come in.

*You are the God of our salvation,
and share your bread with sinners.*

●● Then take the bread,
share the cup:
you are forgiven,
you are accepted,
you are free.

Amen.

We share his peace

Christ is our peace.
He has reconciled us to God
in one body by the cross.

We meet in his name
and share his peace.

The peace of the Lord
be always with you.

And also with you.

Let us offer one another
a sign of peace.

(All may exchange a sign of peace
with a handclasp, saying:
'Peace be with you' . . .
'And also with you'.)

Do this, remembering me

Accept our praise, eternal God, our Father,
through your Son, our Saviour Jesus Christ;
and, as we follow his example and obey his command,
grant that by the power of your Spirit
these gifts of bread and wine
may be for us his body and his blood.

For in the same night that he was betrayed, he
took bread; and after giving you thanks, he broke
it, gave it to his disciples, and said,

'Take, eat; this is my body which is
given for you. Do this, remembering me.'

Again, after supper he took the cup; he gave you
thanks, and gave it to them, saying,

'Drink this, all of you, for this is my blood
of the new covenant which is shed for you and
for many, for the forgiveness of sins. Do this,
as often as you drink it, remembering me.'

(brief silence)

Christ has died.

Christ is risen.

Christ will come again.

Then renew us, our Father, by your Spirit,
inspire us with your love,
and unite us in the body of your Son,
Jesus Christ our Lord.

With him, and in him, and through him,
by the power of the Holy Spirit,
with all who stand before you
in earth and heaven,
we worship you, Father Almighty,
in songs of everlasting praise:

Blessing and honour and glory and power
be yours for ever and ever.
Amen.

Brought together to break bread

The Lord is here.
His Spirit is with us.

Lift up your hearts.
We lift them to the Lord.

Let us give thanks to the Lord our God.
It is right to give him thanks and praise.

It is not only right,
it is our duty and our joy,
at all times and in all places,
to give you thanks and praise, our Father,
almighty and eternal God,
through Jesus Christ,
your only Son, our Lord.

For he is your living Word;
through him you have created
all things from the beginning,
and formed us in your own image.

Through him you have freed us
from the slavery of sin,
giving him to be born as man,
to die upon the cross,
and to rise again for us.

Through him you have made us
a people for your own possession,
exalting him to your right hand on high,
and sending upon us
your eternal and life-giving Spirit.

Accept, then, our praises,
heavenly Father,
through your Son,
our Saviour, Jesus Christ;

And as we follow his example
and obey his command,
grant that by the power of your Spirit
these gifts of bread and wine
may be for us his body and his blood.

For in the same night that he was betrayed,
he took bread; and after giving you thanks,
he broke it, and gave it to his disciples,
and said,

'Take, eat; this is my body
which is given for you.
Do this, remembering me.'

In the same way, he took the cup after supper,
and said,

'Drink this, all of you, for this is my
blood of the new covenant, which is shed
for you and for many, for the forgiveness
of sins. Do this, as often as you drink
it, remembering me.'

Christ has died.

Christ is risen.

Christ will come again.

Amen.

The thanksgiving

The Lord is here.
His Spirit is with us.

Lift up your hearts.
We lift them to the Lord.

Let us give thanks to the Lord our God.
It is right to give him thanks and praise.

All glory and honour, thanks and praise,
be given to you at all times and in all places,
Lord, holy Father, true and living God,
through Jesus Christ our Lord.
For he is your eternal Word
through whom you have created all things
from the beginning,
and formed us in your own image.

In your great love you gave him
to be made man for us, and to share our common life.

In obedience to your will,
your Son, our Saviour, offered himself as a perfect sacrifice,
and died upon the cross for our redemption.

Through him you have freed us from the slavery of sin
and reconciled us to yourself,
our God and Father.

He is our great high priest,
whom you raised from death
and exalted to your right hand on high,
where he ever lives to intercede for us.

Through him you have sent upon us
your holy and life-giving Spirit,
and made us a royal priesthood
called to serve you for ever.

Therefore with angels and archangels
and with all the company of heaven
we proclaim your great and glorious name,
for ever praising you and saying:

Holy, holy, holy Lord, God of power and might,
heaven and earth are full of your glory.
Hosanna in the highest.

Merciful Father, we thank you
for these gifts of your creation, this bread and this wine,
and we pray that we who eat and drink them
in the fellowship of the Holy Spirit
in obedience to our Saviour Christ
and in remembrance of his death and passion
may be partakers of his body and his blood,

    (Taking the bread, the minister says)

who on the night he was betrayed took bread;
and when he had given you thanks
he broke it, and gave it to his disciples, saying,
'Take, eat. This is my body which is given for you.
Do this in remembrance of me.'

    (Taking the cup, the minister says)

After supper, he took the cup,
and again giving you thanks,
he gave it to his disciples, saying,
'Drink from this, all of you.
This is my blood of the new covenant
which is shed for you and for many
for the forgiveness of sins.
Do this, as often as you drink it, in remembrance of me.'

Christ has died;
Christ is risen;
Christ will come again.

Father, with this bread and this cup,
we do as our Saviour has commanded;
we celebrate the redemption he has won for us;
we proclaim his perfect sacrifice
made once for all upon the cross,
his mighty resurrection and glorious ascension;
and we look for his coming
to fulfil all things according to your will.

Renew us by your Holy Spirit,
unite us in the body of your Son,
and bring us with all your people
into the joy of your eternal kingdom;
through Jesus Christ our Lord,
with whom, and in whom,
by the power of the Holy Spirit,
we worship you, Father almighty,
in songs of never-ending praise:

Blessing and honour and glory and power
are yours for ever and ever. Amen.

You have met us in your Son

Father of all,
we give you thanks and praise,
that, when we were still far off,
you met us in your Son and brought us home.
Dying and living, he declared your love,
and gave us grace.

May we who share Christ's body
live his risen life;
we who drink his cup
bring life to others;
we whom the Spirit lights
give light to the world.

Keep us in this hope that we have grasped,
so we and all your children may be free,
and the whole earth live to praise your name.

Through Jesus Christ our Lord.
Amen.

Sounds of the Sacrament

In the awesome name of God,
in the victorious name of Jesus,
in the mysterious name of the Spirit,
we acknowledge our God.

We summon our God,
and we wait.

We are still,
and we wait.

We are silent,
and we wait.

   (brief silence)

We wait for the sounds of God,
and the sounds of the sacrament,

the breaking of bread
and the gushing of wine,

the pain of sorrow
and the pulse of hope,

the echo of our name
and bread in our teeth,

a cup on our lips
and breathing at our side,

a voice in our face:
'The body of your Lord',

a power in our ears:
'The blood of your Lord',

as we wait for the sounds of God,
the sounds of the sacrament,

the breaking of bread
and the gushing of wine.

   (brief silence)

We hear sounds in the distance,
the vibration of human lives,

the crackle of fear
and the murmur of distrust,

the scramble for rice
and the tearing of garbage,

the shuffle of withered limbs
and the breaking of brittle bones,

the shiver of a pregnant mother
and the scream of a motherless child,

the trickle of goat's milk
and the sigh of rich tourists,

the growl of empty bodies
and the splash of spent blood,

the breaking of bread
and the gushing of wine.

   (brief silence)

We hear the snarl of a bullet
and the snap of a trigger,

the thump of lead in flesh
and the bite of steel on bone,

the sudden yell of unseen mines,
the constant moan of riddled skies,

the squeal of angry flames
and the cough of smoking ruins,

the whisper of desolation
and the silence of a lifeless field,

the breaking of bread
and the gushing of wine.

   (brief silence)

We hear the bleating of a lamb
and the breaking of a womb,

the death of a lamb
and the breaking of a tomb.

The beginning of an end
and a word that has healing,

the taste of a mystery
and a God who has feeling,

in the breaking of bread
and the gushing of wine.

(brief silence)

And we will listen for the bursting of joy
and the bubble of children's faces,

the dance of willows
and the surprise of open lives,

the shout of mountains
and the laughter of a second birth,

the leap of our Spirit
and the swirl of celebration,

we will listen to God
and the celebration of God

in the breaking of bread
and the gushing of wine.

The pledge of the Spirit 2 Corinthians 5:5

O God,
You have called us out of death,
we praise you!

Send us back with the bread of life,
we pray you!

You have turned us around,
we praise you!

Keep us faithful,
we pray you!

You have begun a good work,
we praise you!

Complete your salvation in us,
we pray you!

You have made us a chosen people,
we praise you!

Make us one with all people,
we pray you!

You have taught us your law,
we praise you!

Change us by the Spirit's power,
we pray you!

You have sent your Son in one place and time,
we praise you!

Be present in every time and place,
we pray you!

Your kingdom has come in his salvation,
we praise you!

Let it come always among us,
we pray you!

Amen.

Dreams for celebration

Today the Lord steps into the air once more
to taste its colour and feel its songs.
He inhales the thoughts of children,
the breath of yesterday,
the fantasies of tomorrow,
and he wonders whether his children
are too old to celebrate their dreams.

Let us spin him our dreams.

Someday soon people will celebrate life every day.

But we would like to do it now,
wet and wild and risen with our Lord.

Someday soon people will send up balloons in church:

Turn tired old cathedrals into cafeterias:

Paint gravestones as bright as the sun:

Know they are beautiful, black, red, or white:

Glimpse the face of God in their patient parents:

Use the eyes of friends in place of mirrors:

Bounce through the mountains on beachballs:

Write their Christian names in the sunset:

Become as free as that man called Jesus the Christ:

Frolic with the disabled in the park:

Enjoy parties with people in asylums:

Sink their teeth into politics for peace:

Have senses in their souls as sharp as radar:

Send aid and life to the starving:

Love a man because he is a man:

Grow flowers in their garbage can:

Cover their cars with foam rubber:

Turn all bombs into boomerangs:

All bullets into blanks:

And switchblades into tubes of finger-paint:

Slow down and wait for God:

Run through Parliament House with muddy feet:

Laugh with the daffodils in spring:

Dance in the falling autumn leaves:

Baptize their babies with love before birth:

Celebrate Easter as angels do below:

And hang Christmas banners from the moon.

Yes, someday soon people will live like that,
but we plan to start right now.

Right now, Lord. Right now.

Amen, Lord, right now.

3

Advent

You bring me news of a door that opens
at the end of a corridor, sunlight and singing;
when I had felt sure that every corridor
only led to another,
or to a blank wall.

T.S. Eliot

For other prayers and readings
especially suitable for Advent, see
those entitled:

Praise him, all creation 22
Our utmost need 27
The immense longing 29
Pervade us, O God, with your
    presence 33
Attune us to your silence 34

Out of the depths 84
Broken bones may joy 85
Shafts of trust 89
Eternal God and mortal man.... 96
Come, Lord 174

Tomorrows filled with promise

Our God, God of the patriarchs, prophets, and apostles,
of Abraham and Sarah, of Moses, of Hannah,
of Joseph and Mary, of Simeon and Anna, put within us
in this season of Advent the longing for your coming
that was possessed by those who journeyed before us.

*Awaken within us the richness of our origins
and the depths of our past that we may be a
people old in experience and young in hope.*

Come to us as the breaking of the dawn, and dispel
the darkness of our desolation and abandonment
with a sense of expectancy and joy.

*Help us to turn to you with eyes newly open,
with hope reawakened, shrugging off the layers
of care and doubt that have closed about us.*

Lord, prepare us for your coming as pilgrims
of the future, looking for the promise of your
word: the Saviour of the world. Amen.

Mary's song Luke 1:46-55

Tell out, my soul, the greatness of the Lord,
rejoice, rejoice, my spirit, in God my saviour;
so tenderly has he looked upon his servant,
humble as she is.

Yes, from this day forward,
all generations will call me blessed,
for the Almighty has done great things for me.

Holy is his name;
his mercy reaches from age to age
for those who fear him.

The deeds he has done disclose his might,
he has scattered the proud in their conceit.

He has torn imperial powers from their thrones,
and has lifted up the lowly.

The hungry he has satisfied with good things,
and the rich he has sent away empty.

He has come to the help of his servant Israel;
firm in his promise to our ancestors,
he has not forgotten to show mercy to Abraham
and to his descendants for ever.

The insatiable desire

When I dream alone,
that remains a dream;
when we dream together,
that is the beginning of reality.

Helder Camara

• We long, O Lord, to catch hold of a dream,
a vision of yourself
for a world steeped in the darkness of modern times;
a vision of hope,
of strength and of courage,
where so much of what we do gives way
to the persuasion of evil.

•• We see the hurt of those outcast by a society
that cannot tolerate any threat to the norm;
the perplexity of men and women
not understanding a hostile world
in which it is a sin to be different.

• We watch as world leaders
commit the earth's wealth
to strategies of global annihilation,
while thousands remain locked within the walls of poverty,
bound spiritually and physically
by the daily struggle to subsist and survive.

•• We feel the soul-ache of those peoples
wrenched from roots of heritage,
homeland, family, friends,
and alienated from the very centres
that have for centuries been a source
of meaning and understanding,
eternally striving to maintain
the final vestiges of self-esteem,
and always hoping helplessly
for a new future to open before them.

O God,
the hunger for good to prevail becomes
an unbearable agony:
the 'insatiable desire'
for a prism of hope to send its shafts of justice
searing through the present black despair.

- Stir within us the urgency of the prophets;
  inspire your church,
  and fuel this scarred, uncertain Body of Christ
  with new direction,

  So that, by the example of Jesus your Son,
  we will see all men and women
  as through a love-lens
  regardless of race or religion,
  physical or mental capabilities.

  Make us strong in confronting our fears and failures,
  and transform our inadequacies
  into positive expressions of our humanness.

  Let us not settle in shadows of complacency,
  or sit ostrich-like behind our temple curtains,
  but rather search for creative ways
  to channel our discontent.

  Mould us as a community that will dream together,
  struggle toward faith together,
  and, ultimately, be prepared to die together.

  O Father, your creation yearns to be free,
  to be made again in the image of yourself,
  to experience warmth
  amid the cold indifference of our world.

  Spread the dawn-light of your purpose
  over grey horizons;
  enable each to turn
  and fix expectant eyes on you,
  for you alone rise above the imperfections.

  Come, O God,
  your people wait for the day of the Lord.

Dawn for our darkness   Luke 1:68-79

It is written in the book of the prophet Isaiah,
'Look, I am going to send my messenger
before you; he will prepare your way.'

At the birth of John the Baptist, his father
Zechariah was filled with the Holy Spirit and
spoke this prophecy:

Blessed be the Lord, the God of Israel,
for he has turned to his people,
saved them and set them free,
and has raised up a deliverer of victorious
power from the house of his servant David.

So he promised: age after age he proclaimed
by the lips of his holy prophets,
that he would deliver us from our enemies,
out of the hands of all who hate us;
that he would deal mercifully with our fathers,
calling to mind his solemn covenant.

Such was the oath he swore to our father Abraham,
to rescue us from enemy hands,
and grant us, free from fear, to worship him
with a holy worship, with uprightness of heart,
in his presence, our whole life long.

And you, my child, you shall be called
Prophet of the Most High,
for you will go before the Lord
to prepare the way for him;
to give his people knowledge of salvation
through the forgiveness of their sins:

For in the tender mercy of our God
the morning sun from heaven will rise upon us,
to shine on those who live in darkness,
under the cloud of death,
and to guide our feet into the way of peace.

He is one of us

O Lord, our God, when we are afraid,
do not let us despair.

When we are disappointed,
do not let us become bitter.

When we fall,
do not let us remain prostrate.

When we are at the end of our understanding
and our powers, do not let us then perish.

No, let us feel then your nearness and your love,
which you have promised especially to those
whose hearts are humble and broken,
and who stand in fear before your Word.

To all such people everywhere
your Son has come.

Indeed, because not one of us is free
from the afflictions of life,
he was born in a stable and died on a cross.

Lord, awaken us all and keep us awake
to this knowledge and to this confession.

And now we think of all the darkness
and suffering of this our time;

Of the many errors and misunderstandings
with which we torment ourselves;

Of all the burdens that so many
must bear uncomforted;

Of all the great dangers by which our world
is threatened without knowing how
we should meet them.

We think of the sick and the sick in spirit,
the poor, the displaced, and those who suffer injustice;

The children who have no parents,
or no proper parents.

And we think of all who are called to help —
so far as any can help, with the prayer
that the light of Christmas may shine brightly,
much more brightly than before,
for them and for us.

We ask all this in the name of the Saviour,
through whom you have already heard us,
and will hear us again and again.

Amen.

To receive your gift

O Lord, once again you have permitted us
to approach the light, the celebration,
and the joy of Christmas Day;

The day which brings before our eyes
that which is the greatest of all:

Your love, with which you have so loved
the world as to give your only Son,

So that we all might believe in him
and therefore not be lost
but have eternal life.

What then do we have to bring
and give to you?

*The so great darkness in our human relationships
and in our own hearts!*

The so many confused thoughts, so much coldness
and stubborness, so much fickleness and hate!

*So much which separates us from you and one another,
and which certainly does not help us on our way.*

What then can you do with such gifts?
And with such persons as we all are?

*But these are the things you would have from us
at Christmas and would take from us:*

All the refuse and ourselves as well, just as we are,
in order to give us in exchange Jesus our Saviour,

*And in him a new heaven and a new earth,
new hearts and new desires, new clarity
and a new hope, for us and for all people.*

Be among us, as we draw closer
to the celebration of his birth.

*And fill our worship with true and thankful awe,
with expectation and with joy, as we seek together
to prepare ourselves to receive him as your gift.*

The rainbow of our future

- The voice said, 'Come up here,
  and I will show you what will happen hereafter'.

-- At once I was caught up by the Spirit.
  There in heaven stood a throne,
  and on the throne sat one whose appearance was like
  the gleam of jasper and cornelian,
  and round the throne was a rainbow,
  bright as emerald.*

- Lord God, who rules the timeless tracks of eternity,
  the rainbow of your presence assures us of the hope
  which, by your power, stands secure for ever.
  We long for the day when the weapons of our warfare
  will be destroyed and we will all, at last,
  enter into the victory of your peace.

  *Your kingdom come, your will will be done,
  on earth as in heaven.*

-- Lamb of God, who alone can open the scroll of destiny,
  the marks of your slaughter assure us of the love
  which, through your cross, stands secure for ever.
  We look for the day when the tears of suffering humanity
  will be wiped away and we will all, at last,
  enter into the kingdom of your justice.

  *Your kingdom come, your will be done,
  on earth as in heaven.*

- Living Spirit, through whom we experience the joy of the futur
  the reality of your presence assures us of the faith
  which, by your grace, stands secure for ever.
  We live for the day when the bars of our imprisoned existence
  will be torn away and we will all, at last,
  enter into the festival of your freedom.

  *Your kingdom come, your will be done,
  on earth as in heaven.*

* Revelation 4:1-3

Christmas

Child in the manger,
infant of Mary;
outcast and stranger,
Lord of all.

Mary Macdonald

For other prayers and readings
especially suitable for Christmas, see
those entitled:

Put your name upon us 104
Here and now .... 20 A letter not written in ink 125
Good news for celebration .... 23 Sharing 134
Your word and your truth   Belonging 135
  in our midst .... 25 When in prison you came to
Acclaim with joy the depths   my cell 145
  of his love .... 38 Peace prayer of Francis of Assisi 150
Gloria in excelsis .... 40 With what gifts shall we come
Joy comes in the morning 71   before him? 152
In awe and welcome stand ...... 81 The rhythm of community 158

Emmanuel

- Outside Grand Central Station,
a shoe-shine boy was shining shoes.
As he whipped his shine cloth,
again and again,
over his customer's shoes,
a silver medal danced about on his neck.

'Sonny', asked a big man, smoking a cigar,
'What's the hardware around your neck?'

'It's a medal of Mary, the mother of Jesus',
the boy answered.

'But why her medal?' asked the man,
'She's no different, kid,
from your own mother.'

'That's right, Mister',
answered the boy,
'But there's a hell of a difference
between her son and me.'

The big man took a puff from his cigar,
flipped the boy a quarter,
and walked on.

●● 'Mary will bear a son, and you shall give him
the name Jesus, for he will save his people
from their sins.' All this happened
to fulfil what the Lord declared through the
prophet: 'The virgin will conceive and bear
a son, and he shall be called Emmanuel', a
name which means 'God is with us'.

- O Lord, our God,
  who in the birth of your Son Jesus
  has provided our world
  with a great and guiding light
  in the midst of darkness,
  grant that, as we celebrate his birth this day,
  his living presence may create anew:

Grace in our sinfulness,
peace in our strife,
joy in our sadness,
courage in our weakness.

Make it clear to us
that Christ's coming
is your coming;
that his emergence into history
means we will never again
be separated from the love of God.

For this great gift
we give you the wonder of our minds
and the gratitude of our hearts
for ever.

Amen.

Sources: Song of an 'Unpoet'
from *The Merriest Christmas Book;*
Matthew 1:21-23;
prayer by Graeme Garrett

Surprised by joy

- There were some shepherds living in the same part of the
  country, keeping guard throughout the night over their
  flock in the open fields. Suddenly an angel of the Lord
  stood by their side, the splendour of the Lord blazed
  around them, and they were terror-stricken. But the angel
  said to them,

  > 'Do not be afraid! Listen, I bring you
  > glorious news of great joy which is for
  > all the people. This very day, in David's
  > town, a Saviour has been born for you.
  > He is Christ, the Lord. Let this prove
  > it to you: you will find a baby,
  > wrapped up and lying in a manger.'

  And in a flash there appeared with the angel a vast host
  of the armies of heaven, praising God, saying,

  > 'Glory to God in the highest heaven!
  > Peace upon earth among men of goodwill!'

The Gospel of Luke

- ● God does not die on the day when we cease to believe in a
  personal deity, but we die on the day when our lives cease
  to be illumined by the steady radiance, renewed daily,
  of a wonder, the source of which is beyond all reason.

Dag Hammarskjöld

- How surprising that after Winter green shoots
      shoulder their way into the air,
          that after heavy rain, the earth
      panting, clouds melt into white light,
          that after darkness the grasses,
      city buildings and farm fences glow.

  How surprising that it is not at all surprising.

  *O God, who ought to surprise us, take the dullness of our
  apprehending and the smugness of our comprehending, and
  transform them into breathlessness and delight.*

How surprising that our eyes pass over
    a spider's web with silver commas of dew,
    a comical dog glimpsed
    from our bus window,
    the deftness of a small child at hopscotch.

How surprising that our ears do not attend to
    the clean cry of the newspaper seller,
    the shifting of tree branches in high wind,
    the brush of hand across a lover's cheek.

How surprising that it is not at all surprising.

O God, surprise us.

•• At your incarnation, Lord, when you put on our skin and
cried out, it was all so sudden for those who watched.
Make us ready to take your suddenness.

In a flash the angel of the Lord appeared;
in a flash the armies sang.
Let us now go straight to the stable,
let us now be amazed.

••• On the hillsides of our lives, Lord, when the splendour
blazes around us, it is all so sudden for us.
Make us ready to take your suddenness.

In a flash the brightness of your presence comes;
in a flash the world sings.
Let us now go straight to the stable,
let us now be amazed.

Amen.

Christmastide profiles

As Christmas comes round year by year, Lord,
we are tempted to say, 'We have heard
all this so many times before;
we know the story off by heart'.

Forgive us, Lord, and remind us of the difference
between knowing about it, knowing it,
and letting it speak to us again and again.

Help us to see ourselves and our own attitudes
lived out by people in the Christmas story:

The inn-keeper: who couldn't find room
for you in his inn.

Father God, help us cease from cluttering our lives
with countless things — things that don't really
matter; things that crowd you out.

Herod: hostile, jealous, and hating, because
he was afraid of what your coming might do to him.

Lord our God, replace our jealousies
with unselfish joy, our fears with hope,
and our hates with forgiveness.

The shepherds: who were scorned by others
as unskilled labourers, but heard the music
of your coming even while they worked.

Lord, deliver us from the pride that thinks
some tasks too menial, and from prejudices
that blind us to your glory.

The wise men from the east: who journeyed far
to find you.

Teach us again, Eternal God, that those who really
seek will find, and never let us rest content
until we have been found by you.

The grace unspeakable

O Lord, this day with joy
we worship Christ,
God made man.

The announcement of this occurrence
is so unexpected, so great,
it passes knowledge.

Here we stand
at the centre of bright mystery;

Here we confront wonder so large
we cannot contain it;
rather, we are contained by it.

We would have guessed
that, as the eternal, creative Spirit,
your presence, O God, is everywhere and always.

But only in the birth of Jesus
do we find your Spirit
sharing our human existence,
entering our purposes,
bearing our sufferings,
undergoing our death,
accepting our forsakenness.

And in this great reversal of expected roles
we find our hope;

The humanity of God
that restores our lost humanity,

God with us,
that lets us be
with God.

Accept our thanks, O Lord,
for this your grace,
a gift unspeakable in greatness.

Hallelujah for the Christ-child!

- O God,
  how great you are!
  How wonderful the things you do!
  Your actions are so unexpected
  and yet, when eventually we see them,
  we discover how close they are to our world,
  how suited to our situations,
  how compassionate to our needs!

- We would not have guessed
  that your greatest action in history
  is the birth of a baby in Bethlehem.

  And yet it is so.
  And it is so for us.
  For unto us a child is born,
  unto us a Son is given.
  Hallelujah for the Christ-child!

- O God, let the wonder of his birth
  burst brightly across the dark horizon of our life,
  so that routine familiarity does not rob us
  of a part in the glory of this great event.

  Show us the grace of the child-God
  who governs from a cowshed crib;

  Show us the truth of the man-God
  whose wonderful counsel is given
  from a fishingboat at a lakeside;

  Show us the mystery of the crucified-God
  whose might is manifest
  in suffering love from a cross.

Show us the power of the living-God
whose everlasting glory is seen
in resurrection from the grave.

And may the grace
and truth
and mystery
and power
of Christ
flood our history
with a new creation,
the kingdom of God.

• To his name be praise and glory
for ever.

Hallelujah for the Christ-child!

Robert Louis Stevenson's
Christmas Day prayer

- *Let those love now, who never*
  loved before;
  let those who always loved
  *now love the more.**

●● O God, our loving Father,
help us rightly to remember the birth of Jesus,

That we may share in the songs of the angels,
the gladness of the shepherds,
and the worship of the wise men.

May the Christmas morning make us happy
to be your children,

And the Christmas evening bring us to our beds
with grateful thoughts,
forgiving and forgiven, for Jesus' sake.
Amen.

* Anonymous

Year's End and New Year

If only I may become
firmer,
simpler,
quieter,
warmer.

Dag Hammarskjöld

Year's end

O Lord, our God!
Our years come and go,
and we ourselves live and die;
but you remain and are always the same.

Your dominion and your faithfulness,
your righteousness and your mercy,
have no beginning and no end.

And thus you are the origin and the goal
even of our lives; you are the judge
of our thoughts, words, and deeds.

We are grieved that today we can only confess
that even to this hour we have so often
forgotten, denied, and offended you.

But today we are illumined and comforted by the Word
through which you have given us to know
that you are our Father and we are your children —

Because your dear Son, Jesus Christ,
for our sakes has become man,
has died and risen again, and is our brother.

We thank you for the privilege now,
on the last Sunday of the year, of once again
proclaiming and hearing these glad tidings.

Make us free to hear them, receive them, and act
on them, that this hour may serve your glory
and bring to us all peace and well-being.

Amen.

New year

• Our Father and our God,
Creator of life, and Lord of time,
as we stand at the beginning of this new year
we pray that we may stand with you.

You have always been there:
going before us to prepare the way,
standing behind us, urging us on
toward new hopes and a new creation,
being with us in the company of your people
and the life of your Spirit.
You have always been there, Lord,
calling us again to follow you.

•• Help us, today, to see this moment
of New Year as you see it.

Help us to walk quietly and thankfully
away from the old year:

• We thank you for its joys and achievements,
and all the days of growth and love;

*We thank you, too, for strength given amidst
suffering, and hope arising out of fear.*

We are sorry for our mistakes,
for the wrong we could have avoided,
the hurt we have caused.

*We confess our pride,
our greed,
and our failure to love.*

Lord, grant us, we pray,
your judgment of mercy,
your forgiving grace,
even as we forgive one another.

*Let us know your healing power
that we may again be ourselves.*

(pause)

•• Help us, today, to see this moment
of New Year as you see it.

Help us to walk quietly and firmly
toward its opportunities and demands:

• We dare to believe that this is a new day,
and not a repeat of the year now gone.

Your grace gives us courage,
your peace gives us hope.

Your presence is the promise
of new life:

In Christ we can make a new beginning,
in your Spirit we can be a new creation.

•• Lord, we are willing to go with you,
to live the good news of forgiveness
in freedom and joy;
to share the gospel of justice and peace
with courage and love;
to pray with hope and share in faith:

So that all people everywhere
may know your name,
sing your praise,
and share in the joy of your kingdom
in eternal New Year.

Amen.

Epiphany

Those who have nothing can share nothing;
those who are going nowhere
can have no fellow-travellers.

C.S. Lewis

For other prayers and readings
especially suitable for Ephiphany, see
those entitled:

Summons to praise.............. 21
Praise him, all creation 22
Called to serve the cause of right 23
To make your purpose our purpose35
Maker of heaven and earth...... 37
I have called you by name 39

The cosmic Christ............... 44
Life can begin again 46
We do not take an untravelled way69
The divine discontent 122
But not alone 147
The unquenchable hope 149

Beyond what the silent stars tell

● After Jesus had been born at Bethlehem in Judaea
during the reign of King Herod, some wise men came
to Jerusalem from the east. 'Where is the infant king
of the Jews?' they asked. 'We saw his star as it rose
and have come to do him homage.' When King Herod
heard this he was perturbed, and so was the whole of
Jerusalem. He called together all the chief priests and
the teachers of the Law, and enquired of them where
the Christ was to be born. 'At Bethlehem in Judaea',
they told him, 'for this is what the prophet wrote:

> And you, Bethlehem, in the land of Judaea,
> you are by no means least among the leaders of Judah,
> for out of you will come a leader
> who will shepherd my people Israel.'

Then Herod summoned the wise men to see him privately.
He asked them the exact date on which the star had
appeared, and sent them on to Bethlehem. 'Go and find
out all about the child', he said, 'and when you have
found him, let me know, so that I may go and do him
homage.' Having listened to what the king had to say,
they set out. And there in front of them was the star
they had seen rising; it went forward and halted over
the place where the child was. The sight of the star
filled them with delight, and going into the house
they saw the child with his mother Mary, and falling
to their knees they did him homage. Then, opening
their treasures, they offered him gifts of gold
and frankincense and myrrh. But they were warned
in a dream not to go back to Herod, and returned
to their own country by a different way.

●● 'One single beam of his light in our existence
seems to me more important than the full sun
of any orthodoxy. For what is decisive for
all time is not how much we have believed,
but that we have believed and followed him,
however little we may have understood about him.'

Eternal God,
as we come and offer you our worship,
we would remember that in the story of the wise men
Jesus is acknowledged by those who know nothing of God
beyond what the silent stars tell.

Lord, help us move beyond the narrow faith
that wants to confine Jesus to the church,
and fails to see you as Lord of the universe.

Help us possess the humility that is able
to put aside the pride and the fear
which makes us pretend that we know,
and believe what we do not understand.

And as we, like the wise men,
return to the road that goes ever on,
point us beyond its perils
to the horizons of your love
and the purpose of your call.

Amen.

Quotations are from
Matthew 2:1-12
and Ernst Käsemann;
the last two lines
of the first stanza
of the prayer are
from Eduard Schweizer

Light of the world

- Jesus said: 'It is for judgment
  I have come into this world,
  so that those without light may see,
  and those with sight turn blind.'

  Hearing this, some Pharisees who were present said
  to him, 'We are not blind, surely?' Jesus replied:

  'Blind? If you were,
  you would not be guilty;
  but since you say, "We see",
  your guilt remains.'*

  *   *   *

- Without light there is no growth, no discrimination,
  no order, no work, no play, no love.

- Without light there is no human life.

- Day by day, the returning light recreates the world,
  picking it up where it left it yesterday,

- Picking out the loveliness and the scars,
  the beauty and the wrinkles,

- The daffodils and the weeds,
  the comfortable suburb and the slum,
  the cornfields and the battlefields.

- The light restores the memory
  and reveals its limitations;
  it clarifies, defines, and elaborates.

- It can be merciful and merciless,
  according to the situation it reveals,
  according to our readiness for it.

- It adds a new dimension to our life.
  It enriches and complicates it.
  It liberates and betrays us.

- We can walk freely in the light,
  we can dance, we can find our way —
  we are discovered.

* John 9:39-41

- Lord, we must know our blindness
  before we can see; we must see
  before we can understand.

  Forgive our blindness,
  and kindle again the light
  of our hearts and minds.

  Enable us to see our way,
  and to recognize when we are not
  yet on the way.

  Uncover us, and reveal to us
  as much of the truth
  as we can bear.

  Lord, pierce our darkness
  and be the light by which we live,
  today and for ever.

  Amen.

You are accepted

Through many dangers, toils, and snares
  I have already come.
'Tis grace that brought me safe this far,
  and grace will lead me home.

John Newton

Grace strikes us
when we are in great pain and restlessness.

It strikes us
when we walk through the dark valley
of a meaningless and empty life.

It strikes us
when we feel our separation is deeper than usual,
because we have violated another life,
a life which we loved, or from which we were estranged.

It strikes us
when our disgust for our own being,
our indifference, our weakness, our hostility,
and our lack of direction and composure,
have become intolerable to us.

It strikes us
when, year after year, the longed-for
perfection of life does not appear,

When the old compulsions reign within us
as they have for decades,

When despair destroys
all joy and courage.

Sometimes at that moment
a wave of light breaks into our darkness,
and it is as though a voice were saying:

'You are accepted. You are accepted
accepted by that which is greater than you.'

And in that moment, when grace strikes us
and overwhelms us, we are reunited
with that to which we belong and that
from which we are estranged.

(brief silence)

Yes, however great the sin committed,
grace was even greater.
So hear this good news:
you are accepted,
you are forgiven,
you are free.

It is all God's work.

Yes, for God was in Christ
reconciling the world to himself,
not holding men's misdeeds against them.

And he has entrusted us
with this message of reconciliation.

Quotations have been taken
from Romans 5:20
and 2 Corinthians 5:18,19

A surprising start

- It was at this time that Jesus came from Nazareth of Galilee
  and was baptized in the Jordan by John.
  As soon as he came up out of the water,
  he saw the heavens torn apart, and the Spirit,
  like a dove, descending upon him.
  A voice came out of heaven,
      'You are my only Son; on you my favour rests'.*

- - Eternal God,
  creator of the universe,
  ruler of the destiny of nations and of history,
  why did you select such an insignificant and despised
      village as Nazareth?
  why did you choose such an eccentric and outspoken
      rebel as the Baptist?
  why not Rome and the mighty Caesars,
      Jerusalem and the powerful priests?

  *Lord God, forgive us that we attribute such importance
      to the famous and the powerful;
  forgive us that we have failed to discern your presence
      in the out-of-the-way places of the earth;
  forgive us that we have failed to perceive the special
      vocation you have for those who live and work
      on the fringes of our society.*

- - - Eternal Word,
  voice of the prophets,
  source of inspired utterance throughout the ages,
  so often your people believe that the heavens
      have become as unyielding as brass;
  so readily we imagine that you have deliberately separated
      yourself from the struggles of our society;
  so easily, in our travail, we feel that you are no longer
      concerned to communicate with your people.

  *Living Word, we thank you that you resolutely refuse
      to allow our doubts and dogmas to confine you
      to the horizons of heaven;
  we thank you that, in your determination to speak to us,
      you tore apart the barriers of brass, your voice shattering
      the silence of lost eternities;
  we thank you that on the banks of the Jordan
      you openly declared the beginning of a new age
      of revelation in Jesus Christ.*

* Mark 1:9-11

- Eternal Father,
  protector of your people,
  sustainer of life and source of all loving relationships,
  you have fashioned us in your image, creating us to be
      your children;
  you have chosen from among us One destined to be your
  loving Son, eternally seeking to do your will;
  you have appointed him to be the servant and saviour
      of all your people, for ever revealing your reign of grace.

  *Loving Father, help us to discover the destiny for which you
      are preparing us, the vocation for which we were created;
  anoint us with your Spirit, so that, whether we are in
      the wilderness or on the way to Jerusalem,
      we will know your presence among your people;
  strengthen us in your Son so that, irrespective of race,
      colour, or creed, we may serve you in the least of these
      your brothers.*

  Amen.

The morning sun from heaven Luke 1:78

When all within is dark,
and former friends misprise;

From them I turn to you,
and find love in your eyes.

When all within is dark,
and I my soul despise;

From me I turn to you,
and find love in your eyes.

When all your face is dark,
and your just angers rise;

From you I turn to you,
and find love in your eyes.

Where I wander — You!
Where I ponder — You!
Only You, You again, always You!
You! You! You!
When I am gladdened — You!
When I am saddened — You!
Only You, You again, always You!
You! You! You!
Sky is You, earth is You!
You above, You below!
In every trend, at every end,
only You, You again, always You!
You! You! You!

The unexpected at every turn

Almighty God,
as we come to worship and thank you
for the revelation of yourself in Christ,
we come in a spirit of joy and anticipation,
for we know that with you we are liable to
encounter the unexpected at every turn.

We thank you for the fullness of your grace
which is able to break through the barriers between us,
challenging our complacency, dissolving our despair,
and freeing us for the festival of life.

Gracious provider,
when the people of Israel tired of the journey,
murmuring against you and against Moses your servant,
forgetful of your continuing faithfulness to them,
you supplied manna on the morning dew
and in the evening the quails always arrived.

We thank you for sending rain on the just and the unjust,
for, had you supplied our needs according to our merit,
we would have already wasted away in many a wilderness,
dead before gaining even a glimpse of the promised land.

Ever-welcome Guest,
when the hosts at the wedding feast found they had no wine,
and the crowds who followed you neglected to bring the bread,
not knowing that your presence transforms tragedy
into triumph, you revealed your glory and provided
wine of such noble vintage, and bread
in such absolute abundance, that five thousand were fed.

We thank you that your gracious invitation
to share a humble meal transforms our existence,
forgives our folly, and encourages us to continue
in your mission of justice and compassion,
present among people with empty hands and broken hearts.

Father of the unexpected,
to your name be glory and honour,

For ever and ever. Amen.

One Lord, one faith, one hope

• There is one body and one Spirit, just as there is
  one hope held out in God's call to you;
  there is one Lord, one faith, one baptism;
  there is one God and Father of all,
  who is over all and through all and in all.

•• If our love in Christ means anything to you,
  if love can persuade at all,

  Or the Spirit that we have in common,
  or any tenderness and sympathy,

  Be united in your convictions
  and united in your love,

  With a common purpose
  and a common mind.

  Competition and personal vanity
  should have no place among you.

  Rather, be humble toward each other,
  never thinking you are better than others.

• Go into the world in peace,
  be brave, keep hold of what is good,
  never pay back wrong for wrong.

  Support the weak and the distressed,
  give encouragement to each other,
  and seek always to recognize what is best.

  In your life together, and in your
  attitude toward one another,
  be the same as Christ Jesus, your servant Lord.

  For this is what God in Christ
  wills for you.

  He has called you,
  and he will not fail you.

  Amen.

  Ephesians 4:4-6 and selections
  from Philippians 1:10; 2:1-5;
  1 Thessalonians 5:11-24

LENT

To be free, we must be able
to give up what is old,
and so answer God's will
today and tomorrow.

It is hard, church of Jesus, to be a Christian,
for we always have to fight on two fronts:
against the temptation of conforming
to the prevailing patterns of the world;
against the temptation of fashioning Jesus
after our own image.

Ernst Käsemann

For other prayers and readings
especially suitable for Lent see those
entitled:

Worship without pretence 24
Testing the promise by living the
  hope 25
Mercy and freedom are his gifts . 26
Where many paths and errands
  meet 30
Because you believe in us 32
Come away 35
Our call and commission 58
The community of grace 61
Patience that waits our returning 73
Recognizing the bonds 75
Jesus 100
Beyond all pretence 103
Put your name upon us 104
Tensed against tenderness 110
Steps marking our way 119

The promise of your presence... 123
In all things be our strength ... 124
Courage to change 132
When in prison you came to my
  cell 145
Whatsoever you do 153
Find your love 154
Where your treasure is 155
Against the wind 156
Venturing the harder road 164
Between already and not yet ... 170
Our ultimate loyalty 172
The scandal of grace 178
Transformed nonconformist 322
Fortitude 326
Happiness is 328

Where the Spirit of the Lord is, there is freedom 2 Corinthians 3:17

- 'The gift of freedom remains ours only as long as we are constantly renewing our efforts to reach it, as those who are waiting and receiving the first beatitude. It is enough that we reach out, with the world, for his freedom, and let it consecrate us.'*

•• God our Father, you are maker of heaven and earth:

Be our freedom, Lord!

God the Son, you redeem us all:

Be our freedom, Lord!

God, Holy Spirit, comforter and disturber:

Be our freedom, Lord!

* Ernst Käsemann

God, one God, beyond understanding,
made known in Jesus, present in our midst:

Be our freedom, Lord!

By your incarnation and your birth in poverty,
by your baptism, your fasting and trials in the desert:

Be our freedom, Lord!

By your agony in the garden, by your cross and passion,
by your death and your burial, by your resurrection
and ascension, and by the gifts of your Holy Spirit:

Be our freedom, Lord!

In times of trouble, and when all goes well,
at the hour we die, and on the day of your glory:

Be our freedom, Lord!

From war and violence, from hardness of heart,
and from contempt of your love and your promises:

Be our freedom, Lord!

Enlighten our lives with your Word, that in it
we may find our way and our hope:

Be our freedom, Lord!

Assist your people in every land, govern them in peace
and justice, defend them from the enemies of life:

Be our freedom, Lord!

The simplicity of the carefree life Matthew 6:25-34

- 'So do not be anxious about tomorrow;
  tomorrow will look after itself.
  Each day has troubles enough of its own.'

  Jesus

•• We have been seduced, Lord,
  trapped into an unthinking alliance with this world's powers,
  deceived into insuring our lives against some fateful day.

  We have sought security
  in the food in our pantries,
  the cars in our garages,
  and the money in our bank accounts.
  Houses, clothes, and jobs have stolen our time and energy.
  Lovingly we have lavished money and attention
  upon commodities of our market places
  and the business houses of our cities.

  Your words are plain, Lord:
  there is no cause for confusion.
  Yet it seems they have fallen upon deaf ears.
  Too easily we have sought to sweep them aside,
  explaining them away as beautiful sentiments,
  but naive,
  impractical,
  unrealistic for the modern world in which we live.
  Worst of all, we have labelled them foolish.

  It is we who are the foolish ones, Lord,
  for we have become enmeshed in a world of nations
  frantic in their struggle for economic superiority,
  insane in their clamour for destructive weapons,
  as if their very possession could guarantee a future
  free for ever from fear and want.

- Teach us, Lord,
  that our insatiable hunger for security
  can be satisfied only by you.

  Liberate us from a misdirected search for comfort
  that blinds us to the lasting values of life
  and causes us to treat men and women as
  means to an end.

Discipline our desires
that we may not pursue an unchecked quest for acquisitions
which will inevitably encumber us in our faith
and hamper us in our mission.

Save us, Lord,
from anxiety about tomorrow,
and fears of the unknown
which render us impotent to live
and work for you in the present.
Release us from the burdens
which are not ours to carry.

Free us, Lord,
from the mistaken belief
that we are the ones appointed to save the world.

Affirm in us the faith
that Christ alone is saviour,
and that we, for our part, are Followers of the Way.

With the assurance of your words,
help us to be so confident of your fatherly love
that we may learn to live in dependence upon you
and in community with our brothers and sisters.

Remind us, Lord,
that in the simplicity of the carefree life
we may discover Christ,
who had nowhere to lay his head.

May anxiety and care be banished for ever
to the glory of your holy name.

Amen.

Choices

Lord, in this world of mixed and changing values,
we ask for others, for each other, and for ourselves,
the wisdom to distinguish between
the important and the unimportant,
the true and the false,
the trivial and the eternal.

Sometimes we do not know which way to turn.
There are many claims upon our time,
so many demands for our attention.

Life pulls us in many directions,
and presents many possibilities,
so that the very range of choices before us
can help to confuse rather than clarify.

It is then that we need you,
for yours is the ultimate claim on our lives.

Help us to listen for it in all the other claims
that are made on us.

Because we cannot do everything,
help us to get our priorities right,

To know what you want us to do now,
and what we have to leave.

And, as we seek to be your disciples,
help us to see that what we do,
and what we allow your Spirit to do
with everything that happens to us:

With the foreseen and the unexpected,
with delights and trials,
with criticism and praise,
with good fortune and grief,

Will shape what we will become.

Amen.

The cost of discipleship

Are you able to drink the cup that I drink?
Mark 10:38

Heavenly Father,
we have decided for your kingdom
and dared to take your cup.

But we confess that we do not understand
the fearsome consequences of obedience.

When we are brought to the test,
steady our nerve and hold us in our faith,

That we may sail through heavy seas,
and ride the frightening storm.

Through Jesus Christ, our Lord.

Amen.

The true wilderness

The path is a long one,
strewn with mistakes,
tentative steps, injustice,
and the cries — not only of anguish,
but also of love,
compassion, and exultation.

Lord, they were the people you had set free,
they had believed in you, the exodus God,
but now in the desert they were lost.

Day followed day in a succession
of frustrations, anxieties, and difficulties.

Some wanted to return to slavery
responding to the lure of the familiar.
Some were content to complain in the wilderness,
to resign from the struggle to journey on.

They could follow no more
the call to an unproved land.

The disciples, treading the road
to Jerusalem with Jesus,
felt the chill of deepening shadows;
the anger of the religious,
the fear of the politicians,
the hurt pride of the traditionalists.

What lay ahead?
They were bewildered, uncertain.

We, Lord, who call ourselves your people,
share the wilderness and the road.
We set out in great hope,
sure of our God
and of the path ahead.

But now our dreams are shattered,
we are disappointed and perplexed,
too weary to be angry,
struggling to find reason
in a world of pain, competition, and hate.

We, too, would go back;
but deep in our hearts we know
that time has gilded the past,
heightened the joys but dimmed reality.
We cannot go back,
and the future we cannot see.

God of the exodus,
when we lose sight of you,
and are on the point of turning back,
remind us that, although in this life
we will never arrive,
it is on the road that you meet us,
and to your future that you call us.

Remind us, too, that it is in the desert
that we have experienced your grace
and have grown stronger and gentler.

For, to those who persist and journey on,
there is the surprise of discovering
that the desert is fertile.

Temptation Matthew 4:1-10

• Then Jesus was led up by the Spirit into the wilderness to be tempted by the devil. He fasted forty days and forty nights, and afterward he was hungry. The tempter came and said to him, 'If you are the Son of God, command these stones to become loaves of bread.'

Jesus answered, 'It is written,
"Man shall not live by bread alone,
but by every word that proceeds from the mouth of God".'

•• Then the devil took him to the holy city, and set him on the pinnacle of the temple, and said to him, 'If you are the Son of God, throw yourself down; for it is written, "He will give his angels charge of you, and on their hands they will bear you up, lest you strike your foot against a stone".'

Jesus said to him, 'Again it is written,
"You shall not tempt the Lord your God".'

••• Again, the devil took him to a very high mountain, and showed him all the kingdoms of the world in all their glory, and he said to him, 'All these I will give you, if you fall down and worship me.'

Jesus said to him, 'Get out of here, Satan;
for it is written, "You shall worship the Lord
your God and him only shall you serve".'

- Eternal God, creator of the universe,
  the temptation to win back the world
  by sending a mighty miracle-working Messiah
  must present a perennial problem, even for you.

  We confess that our endless quest for possessions
  so often outweighs our hunger and thirst for justice,
  that we are frequently tempted to forfeit our future
  so that we might feast at the table of technology.

  Father, lead us not into temptation,
  but deliver us from evil.

•• Lord Christ, redeemer of mankind,
  the temptation to win back the world
  by a magnificent display of daring
  must present a perennial problem, even for you.

  We confess that our craving for acclaim
  so often outweighs our commitment to the cross
  that we are frequently tempted to sacrifice our souls
  so that we might taste the sweet savour of success.

  Father, lead us not into temptation,
  but deliver us from evil.

••• Holy Spirit, strength of your people,
  the temptation to win back the world
  by the exercise of coercive political power
  must present a perennial problem, even for you.

  We confess that our desire to dominate
  so often outweighs our will to participate in your mission
  that we are frequently tempted to turn from the paths of peace
  so that we might enjoy the transitory spoils of war.

  Father, lead us not into temptation,
  but deliver us from evil,
  for yours is the kingdom, the power, and the glory,
  for ever and ever. Amen.

Vision and mirage

- Lord Jesus, you have faced temptation;
  you know how difficult it can be
  to distinguish between vision and mirage,
  between truth and falsehood.

•• Lord, help us when we are tempted:

And save us when we fall.

- Help us in the church:
  when we confuse absence of conflict with the peace of God;
  when we equate the shaping of ecclesiastical structures
  with serving you in the world;
  when we imagine that our task is to preserve
  rather than to put at risk;
  when we behave as though your presence in life
  were a past event rather than a contemporary encounter.

•• Lord, help us when we are tempted:

And save us when we fall.

- Help us in the world:
  when we use meaningless chatter to avoid real dialogue;
  when we allow the image presented by the media
  to blind us to the substance that lies behind it;
  when we confuse privilege with responsibility, and claim
  rights when we should acknowledge duties;
  when we allow high-sounding reasons to cover evil actions.

•• Lord, help us when we are tempted:

And save us when we fall.

- We pray for all who have been brought
  to the edge of their endurance;
  for those whose pain is unending;
  for those for whom the earth is a cruel desert
  and existence a constant struggle
  against overwhelming odds;
  for those who suffer through their own folly
  or through the malice or folly of others.

•• Lord, help us when we are tempted:

And save us when we fall.

- Lord Jesus, you have passed through the test of suffering,
  and are able to help those who are meeting their test now.

•• Lord, help us when we are tempted:

And be with us to the end.

Doing the truth

- What then of the man who hears these words of mine
  and acts upon them?
  He is like a man who had the sense
  to build his house on rock.
  The rain came down, the floods rose,
  the wind blew, and beat upon that house —
  but it did not fall,
  because its foundations were on rock.
  But what of the man who hears these words of mine
  and does not act upon them?
  He is like a man who was foolish enough
  to build his house on sand.
  The rain came down, the flood rose,
  the wind blew, and beat upon that house —
  and down it fell with a great crash.

- - The only proper response to this word which Jesus
  brings with him from eternity is simply to do it.
  Only in the doing of it does the word of Jesus
  retain its honour, might, and power among us.
  Now the storm can rage over the house,
  but it cannot shatter that union with him,
  which his word has created.

- 'Yes, if you make my word your home,
  you will indeed be my disciples;
  you will learn the truth,
  and the truth will make you free'.

•• Eternal God, in Jesus
you have shown us how to do the truth.

But we confess that still we substitute
words for action
and busyness for reflection.

So often we delude ourselves into thinking
that what we believe
is more important than how we believe.

You ask us to have tough minds and tender hearts;
but too often it is our minds that are tender
and our hearts that are tough.

Help us, O God, to understand that to respond
to the good news about you and from you
is to act, to be changed, to become a new being.

Help us to really hear the words of Jesus
so that you might bring us
into your new kingdom.

Amen.

Sources:
Matthew 7:24-27
Dietrich Bonhoeffer
John 8:31,32

Forgiveness

Lord, we find it so easy to talk about forgiveness —
but so difficult to accept it for ourselves.
We know our need, Lord.
We know our need for newness of life;
confession comes readily to us — and yet
so little changes.

Lord, we are afraid.
We want your forgiveness, but we fear being known.
There are those things within us which we prefer to hide,
deep shadows vaguely sensed.
There are those things we know too well about ourselves,
and things we dare not know.
Without our being known there is no forgiveness for us,
and so we are afraid.

Lord, give us the courage to accept your forgiveness,
and so to grow into our promised newness.
Lord, forgive us.

Lord, we would be free:
free from bondage to our own past,
and free from the past of our community.
Take us into your future, O God,
with the power that comes with freedom;
renew us as creatures and as creators
that we may face our world with new possibility
in the power that is forgiveness.

The new commandment

- You shall have no gods except me.
  You shall not make yourselves a graven image. . .
  You shall not take the name of the Lord
  lightly on your lips. . .
  Remember the Sabbath day and keep it holy. . .
  Honour your father and your mother. . .
  You shall not kill.
  You shall not commit adultery.
  You shall not steal.
  You shall not bear false witness
  against your neighbour.
  You shall not covet anything
  that is your neighbour's.

- And Jesus said:
  'I give you a new commandment:
  love one another;
  just as I have loved you,
  you also must love one another.'

  Then let us love one another,
  since love comes from God,
  and everyone who loves
  is begotten by God and knows God.

  Anyone who fails to love
  can never have known God,
  because God is love.

  God's love for us was revealed
  when God sent the world his only Son
  so that we could have life through him.

  This is the love I mean:
  not our love for God,
  but God's love for us
  when he sent his Son
  to be the sacrifice that takes
  our sins away.

God is love,
and anyone who lives in love lives in God,
and God lives in him.
Love will come to its perfection in us
when we can face the day of judgment
without fear,
because even in this world
we have become as he is.

In love there can be no fear,
but fear is driven out by perfect love;
because to fear is to expect punishment,
and anyone who is afraid
is still imperfect in love.

We are to love, then,
because he loved us first.

Anyone who says, 'I love God',
and hates his brother,
is a liar,
since a man who does not love
the brother that he can see,
cannot love God,
whom he has never seen.

So this is the commandment
that he has given us,
that anyone who loves God
must also love his brother.

Exodus 20:1-17
John 13:34
1 John 4:7-10; 16-21

Shadows of fear

Those who followed were afraid.
Mark 10:32

Eternal God,
we have answered your call, and have said
that we will follow you.

And now we are afraid
that we have involved ourselves in a life
that is too much for us.

Help us to a firmer resolution,
to follow our Lord so closely
that life shall not crowd him from sight.

And, as we keep him in view,
put strength in our feet and joy in our heart.

The darkness is never so distant

In Germany they came first for the Communists, and
I didn't speak up because I wasn't a Communist.
Then they came for the Jews, and I didn't speak up
because I wasn't a Jew. Then they came for the
trade unionists, and I didn't speak up because I
wasn't a trade unionist. Then they came for the
Catholics, and I didn't speak up because I was a
Protestant. Then they came for me — and by that
time no one was left to speak up.

Pastor Martin Niemöller

(to be read in silence)

• We judge other generations for their folly
and their blindness, we recoil from
their prejudice and inhumanities
and condemn them for their indifference,

While in our own days the dark wings of evil
cast a colder, longer shadow
and sweep much nearer to us
than we want to perceive or care to admit.

•• Lord, deliver us from the dishonest conscience,
that is chilled by the cruelties of yesterday,
shudders at the evils on a distant shore,

*But feels no shame — not even a blush —
has no eyes, no ears, no heart,
for the undressed wounds within our reach.*

Lord, give us the will and strength
to turn and face the realities of evil
in our own time:

*To see that wherever hatred, revenge
or injustice are dominant,
evil is actively at work;*

To perceive that where bitterness and despair
exercise their paralysing power
over the hearts of men and women,

*And take from them the courage to make
a new beginning in your name,
there, too, evil is at work;*

To acknowledge that nothing good
can come out of these things,
for they must always lead to annihilation.

*Lord, preserve us from deceptions that corrode
all integrity, from fears that masquerade
behind facades of rational explanations.*

Lord, save us from the religion that is no more
than a form of rebellion against you
because it uses your Word to hide from reality.

Amen.

When little is left

Lord, we embrace in our prayers today those who live
with a sense of running out of what they need:

Those who are running out of time,
their dreams still unfulfilled;

Those who are running out of patience,
wondering how they can endure;

Those who are running out of health,
who feel their powers waning day by day;

Those who are running out of money,
fighting growing costs on fixed incomes;

Those who are running out of excuses, nearing the time
when they must assume the blame for their failures;

Those who are running out of faith, having borrowed
too much and too long from others;

Those who are running out of love, finding it easier
all the time to accuse and criticize and hate.

O Lord, able to keep us from falling
if only we put our trust in you:

Where our reserves are low, fill us again,
for we would endure all the way to the end.

Amen.

The threshold

There is a threshold, it seems,
where either the spirit cracks
or some steel enters the soul.

Graeme Barrett

God our Father, when the foundations of our life
are shaken by the bitter winds of disappointment,
or by a grief that seems too great to bear,
take hold of us and help us through to the other side.

And should there come the day when we must
stand firm against the forces of evil, or say No
to a demand that we sell our soul, help us
not be broken by the consequences of our decision
or action, even though a dream we followed
lies in fragments at our feet.

Lord, take all that happens to us and turn it
to good account, so that the furnace of adversity
may in the end succeed only in deepening our trust,
lengthening our cords of sympathy,
and widening the horizons of our world.

Amen.

To the end

He set his face resolutely toward Jerusalem.
Luke 9:51

● No, do not give in.
Grace divine
was your good beginning.
That grace is greater
which does not falter.
But the greatest
is to keep going,
however
you are undermined,
to endure,
however harassed,
to the end.

●● We bless you, Father
for the thirst
you put in us,

For the boldness
you inspire,

For the fire
alight in us —

That is you in us,
you the just.

Never mind
that our thirst
is mostly unquenched
(pity the satisfied).

Never mind
our bold plots
are mostly unclinched,
wanted, not realized.

Who better than you
knows that success
comes not from us?

You ask us to do
our utmost only,
but willingly.

Passiontide

There are some things
it is better to begin
than to refuse
even though the end
may be dark.

J.R.R. Tolkien

For other prayers and readings
especially suitable for Passiontide,
see those entitled:

I have betrayed .... 98 A world in which faith comes
You shall know the truth 102   hard 144
Father, forgive .... 105 Redemptive suffering 168
Take fire .... 116 Given for the life of the world .. 180

259

Who takes away the sin of the world John 1:29

O Saviour of the world,
who by your cross
and precious blood
has redeemed us:

*Save us and help us,
we pray, and loose us
from our sins.*

O Lamb of God,
who takes away the sin of the world,
have mercy on us.

*O Lamb of God,
who takes away the sin of the world,
grant us your peace.*

O Lamb of God,
who takes away the sin of the world,
receive our prayer.

Amen.

Jesus our Lord

Let us think on Jesus the Lord:
instead of the joy meant for him,
he endured the cross, ignoring its disgrace.

We worship you, Lord, upon the cross.

O Jesus Christ, the King of glory,
born in humility to confound the proud
and to raise the humble, you became
the poor workman of Nazareth
to teach us true wealth:

We worship you, Lord, upon the cross.

You went among us, doing good,
proclaiming the good news to the poor
and freedom to prisoners:

We worship you, Lord, upon the cross.

You came to loose the chains
of every slavery,
friend of the humble,
bread of hungry souls,
healer of the sick:

We worship you, Lord.

Jesus, pattern of patience and goodness,
prophet of the kingdom of God,
Master, gentle and humble of heart,
forgiving all who loved much,
and calling the weary and the burdened:

We worship you, Lord.

Jesus, you came into the world
to serve and to lay down your life;
you had nowhere to lay your head;
you were betrayed for money,
dragged before Pilate,
and nailed to the cross:

We worship you, Lord.

Jesus, Lord of all the worlds
by your resurrection from the dead,
alive for ever to intercede
with your Father and ours:

We worship you.

The centre of the mystery of the Christ

Christ died for us while we were yet sinners,
and that is God's own proof of his love
toward us.
Romans 5:8

The Christ had to suffer and die,
because, whenever the Divine appears in all its depths,
it cannot be endured by men.

It must be pushed away
by the political powers,
the religious authorities,
and the bearers of cultural tradition.

In the picture of the Crucified,
we look at the rejection of the Divine
by humanity.

Yet when the Divine is rejected,
it takes the rejection upon itself.

It accepts our crucifixion,
our pushing away,
the defence of ourselves against it.

It accepts our refusal to accept,
and thus conquers us.

That is the centre
of the mystery
of the Christ.

Good Friday

O love of God! O sin of man!
In this dread act your strength is tried,
and victory remains with love,
for he, our Lord, is crucified.

F.W. Faber

For other prayers and readings
especially suitable for Good Friday,
see those entitled:

Your love is strong enough 72
You shall know the truth 102
Failed 114
Penitence 115
Take fire...................... 116
Enough! 120
The Word was made flesh 127
Love which leads to awareness . 139
Peace prayer of Francis of Assisi 150
Just as we are 181
Love's as warm as tears........ 335

Ours were the sorrows he carried Isaiah 52:13 — 53:12

● Listen to this: my servant will prosper,
he shall be lifted up, exalted, rise to great heights.

As many were aghast at his appearance
— so disfigured did he look
that he seemed no longer human —
so will many nations recoil at the sight of him,
and kings stand speechless before him;
for they shall see what they have never been told,
and things unheard before will fill their thoughts.

●● Who would believe what we hear,
and to whom has the Lord's power been revealed?
For he grew up before him as a sapling,
as a root from dry ground;
he had no form or dignity that would have pleased us,
no appearance to which we would be attracted;
he was despised and rejected by men,
tormented and humbled by suffering,
a person from whom people hid their faces.

He was despised;
we thought him of no account;
but ours were the sufferings he bore,
ours the sorrows he carried.
We thought him stricken,
smitten by God and afflicted;
but he was pierced for our transgressions,
crushed for our iniquities;
the chastisement bringing us welfare was on him,
and by the stripes he bore there was healing for us.

Like sheep we had all gone astray,
each of us turning to his own way,
and on him the Lord laid the guilt of us all.
He was harshly treated,
but he bore it humbly,
and did not open his mouth.
As a sheep that is led to the slaughter,
as a ewe before her shearers is dumb,
so he did not open his mouth.

After arrest and trial he was taken away,
but who gave a thought to his fate,
that he was cut off from the land of the living,
stricken to death for the transgression of my people?
Among the wicked was his grave,
among the mob was his burial place,
although he had practised no violence,
no deceit was in his mouth.

But the Lord was pleased with his afflictions:
he will heal him who put forward his life
as a guilt offering;
he will enjoy posterity, with life prolonged,
and the Lord's purpose will prosper under his charge.
After his sorrowful labours he will see light,
and be satisfied with his knowledge.

• My Servant shall vindicate many,
and their iniquities he shall bear.
Therefore I will set him among the great,
and he shall divide the spoil with the mighty,
because he surrendered himself to death,
and was counted among transgressors,
by bearing the sin of many,
by standing in the place of transgressors.

The safest response to the surprising God?

- The truth and glory of Easter
  is to be found only in the cross.

  *It is in the crucified Christ
  that we see the God who
  suffers with and for his people.*

  It is the cross which shows us
  that there is nothing God will not face,
  will not endure at the hands of his own people.

  *But Jesus on the cross reveals not only God;
  we also see ourselves for what we really are.*

  Judas: for whom money is more important
  than any relationship; perhaps the zealot who
  hopes to force Jesus' hand and manipulate
  him into supporting his own ideology.

  *Caiaphas: with his impeccable political
  and ecclesiastical logic that 'it is better
  for one man to die for the people'.*

  Pilate: the victim of circumstance —
  on the opposite side of the debate to Caiaphas
  but playing the same rules: someone's head must
  roll; if not that of Jesus, it will be his own.

  *The cynical witnesses: who remembered only
  the incriminating words and forgot the message.*

  Peter: with his inappropriate
  self-confidence.

  *The crowd: in its mindless
  thirst for blood.*

  The soldiers: in their
  casual brutality.

  *The centurion: who admired
  from a distance.*

  The disciples: who ran away.

Lord Jesus, we are all there,
we are all part of this human drama;
there is a part in all of us
which still says that the safest response
to the surprising God is to kill him
while we have a chance:

•• To get him out of our lives,
to make him leave us alone;
to be rid of him so we can have
the security of our preferred politics,
our cosy religion, our national interests.

Lord God, help us this Easter
not to run away, but to face the truth
that our sin is more complicated,
more insidious, more devastating
than we ever dreamed:

And that your grace reaches out
to overcome it;

That our human brokenness
makes even our best aspirations
potentially disastrous,

But that you will take
our every aspiration and transform it,
will take us and make us co-workers
with you, if we are willing
to come to the cross and
learn the truth.

Good Friday

- Lord, truly you have borne our griefs
  and carried our sorrows.
  On this most terrible and wonderful day,
  when the sun was dimmed
  and the earth shuddered in horror,
  we know it.

- Lord, no longer is it only the blood of our brother
  that cries out from the ground.
  Today we hear the voice of the blood of God
  pleading from the soil
  with a claim which will never be silenced
  nor ever defeated.

Lord, everywhere we go your holy blood speaks:
from the rocky soil of Israel,
the green fields of Devon and the vineyards of the Rhine,
out of the clays of Uganda,
from the prairies of Canada and rice paddies of Vietnam:
the cry of love.

Lord, our homeland, too, shudders in loving recognition,
everywhere is now Golgotha:
Yanchep and Wilpena, Gove, Burnie, and Kingaroy,
sheep stations and dairy farms,
Blue Mountains and Wimmera wheatlands,
all cry with the blood of the crucified God.

Lord, if in love we offered you our homeland,
it would be poor thanks;
if the whole wealth of Mother Earth were given,
even that would be inadequate praise.
O you who bear our griefs and carry our sorrows,
we are yours!

Forsaken?

● My God! My God, why have you forsaken us —
forsaken us in the cry of the crucified!
In his horrible helplessness
we are doubly helpless,
suffering by the million
and dying
alone.

My God! The nails that pierced Jesus cruelly
surely pierce our one humanity;
the taunts from bystanders are ours:
the secret doubt that all
ends in an empty whimper,
bereft of light and
love.

My God! That his life should thus mercilessly end,
surrounded by such malignant rejection,
loved only by a frightened few
watching in fear,
leaves us all in
dereliction and
despair.

My God! Into that cold stone tomb
fall all our noblest human dreams;
the idealism of youth sinks
low in the deep shadows,
and even desperate defiance
in the darkness
weeps.

•• Dear God! On that black Friday you did not forsake us!
Not Jesus, nor any other desolate child of man!
That day you entered all our forsakenness,
tasting bitter dereliction and death,
shaping the valley of the shadow
to become an avenue of
hope.

We praise you, O God! We acknowledge you to be the Lord!
Despised and rejected, man of sorrows and grief,
great and marvellous are your deeds!
Wounded for our transgressions,
bruised for our iniquities,
God is with us!
Hallelujah!

Delivered to death for our misdeeds   Romans 4:25

Saviour,
you have conquered tears by your crying,
pain by your suffering,
and death by your dying.

We come together before your cross
to remember your suffering
and to realize afresh the wonder
of your compassion and love.

As we listen to your words from the cross,
show us the truth about ourselves.

Let us know, and help us acknowledge,
what our sins have done.

And let us determine
to follow your way of life,
bringing glory to your name for ever.
Amen.

Easter

The resurrection is
God's 'Yes'
to the words and deeds, the suffering and death
of Jesus from Nazareth.

Terry Falla

For other prayers and readings
especially suitable for Easter, see
those entitled:

The call of freedom has been
  sounded 21
There is a new world 43
The cosmic Christ............... 44
Life can begin again 46
The meaning of Providence 48

Risen and still with you 52
Cosmic hymn of praise 82
Sounds of the Sacrament 190
The pledge of the Spirit 193
Dreams for celebration 194

Confessions at the empty tomb

Lord, Jesus Christ,
we come to express our feelings.

We come with anxiety and sorrow,
with hope and expectation.

Lord, Jesus Christ,
we come to the lonely cross:

And we see you stripped,
we see you murdered,
we see you deserted.

Lord, Jesus Christ,
we come to the empty tomb:

And we see our own death,
we see our own tomb,
we see our own emptiness.

Lord, Jesus Christ,
when we come to the empty tomb:

We remember how we treated
our parents,
our friends,
our neighbours,
our Lord —
and we feel sorry
for ourselves.

Lord, Jesus Christ,
when we come to the empty tomb:

We see a hungry world before us,
the pain of starving children,
the guilt of war on our hands,
the terror of friends without rights —
and we know that we share in these evils.

Lord, Jesus Christ,
when we come to the empty tomb:

We search inside ourselves
and we cannot escape what we are:
men caught in our selfish love,
our cold hypocrisy,
our depressions,
our loneliness,
and our frustrations.

Lord, Jesus Christ,
when we come to the empty tomb:

We face you as never before,
as the one forgotten,
as the one oppressed,
as the one pushed aside,
as the one left out.

Lord, Jesus Christ,
we come to the empty tomb:

To confess our guilt,
our pain,
our emptiness,
and to look for hope from you.

Healings from the empty tomb

- Men of God,
  why do you seek the living
  among the dead?

  Because we are afraid,
  we are uncertain,
  we are uncomfortable here,
  and we have doubts about this man.

•• Do not be afraid,
  for he has risen from the dead,
  he has broken through the tomb,
  he has come back to life,
  and he is here among us now.

- Men of God,
  why do you seek the living
  among the dead?

  Because we feel guilty,
  we feel lonely,
  and we feel lost,
  for we deserted that man.

•• Do not carry your guilt any longer,
  for he has taken the guilt himself,
  he has buried it in his grave,
  he has lifted it to his cross,
  and he is here among us now.

- Men of God,
  why do you seek the living
  among the dead?

  Because our wounds are deep.
  We have torn away from that man,
  we have broken with him
  and with our fellowmen.

•• Do not dwell on your wounds
for he has risen to heal you,
he has risen to forgive you,
he has risen to change you all,
and bind us all together now.

• Men of God,
he is not here; he is risen.

Yes, he is risen!

He is risen!

And he is here!

Alleluia!

Alleluia!

He is risen!

And he is here!

Crucified risen one!

Lord Jesus,
we greet you, risen from the dead,
victorious over sin and death,
over suffering and shame,
over all evil and wrong.

Lord Jesus,
we greet you, risen from the dead,
overcoming by the power of love,
by patient trust and perseverance,
by faith in God alone.

Lord Jesus,
we greet you, risen from the dead,
proving that nothing can separate us from God's love,
showing us how far that love will go,
and suffering for the sins of the world.

Lord Jesus,
we greet you, risen from the dead,
and offer you our thanks and our praise,
our prayers and our worship,
our devotion and our service for ever.

Through the flames of heaven

• Universe
and every universe beyond,
spin and blaze,
whirl and dance,
leap and laugh
as never before.

•• It's happened!
It's new!
It's here!
The liberation.
The victory.
The new creation.

Christ has smashed death!
He has liberated the world!
He has freed the universe!

*You and I and everything
are free again,
new again,
alive again!*

Let's have a festival
and follow him across the skies,
through the flames of heaven
and back down every alley of our town.

*There, let's have him come
to liberate our city,
clean up the mess
and start all over again.*

You conquered.
Keep on fighting through us.
You arose.
Keep on rising in us.
You celebrated.
Keep on celebrating with us.
You happen.
You are new.
You are here.

Pentecost

The Holy Spirit is totally primordial.
His is the elemental force beyond
all other forces,
and to call it, correctly,
the force of love
is not to temper its intensity
but to increase fearfully
our estimate of love's fervour.

John V. Taylor

For other prayers and readings
especially suitable for Pentecost, see
those entitled:

Here and now.................... 20
Good news for celebration 23
To make your purpose our purpose35
Let the winds of the Spirit 36
Our mission in the world 63
That dreams may be dreamt ... 121
Using our gifts.................. 159
Between already and not yet ... 170
The pledge of the Spirit 193

More than we can measure or imagine
Ephesians 3:14-21

I kneel in prayer to the Father,
from whom every family in heaven
and on earth takes its name,

That out of the treasures of his glory
he may grant you strength and power
through his Spirit in your inner being,
that through faith Christ may dwell
in your hearts in love.

With deep roots and firm foundations,
may you be strong to grasp,
with all God's people,

What is the breadth and length
and height and depth of the love of Christ,

And to know it,
though it is beyond knowledge.

So may you attain to fullness of being,
the fullness of God himself.

Now to him who is able to do immeasurably more
than all we can ask or imagine,
by the power which is at work among us,

To him be glory in the church and in Christ Jesus
from generation to generation evermore! Amen.

Breath of our life

You are built upon the foundation
laid by the apostles and prophets,
the cornerstone being
Christ Jesus himself.
Ephesians 2:20

Eternal God, holy Father,
our origin, our destiny, depth of our being,
breath of our life, who ever delights
in the worship and service of your children,
be pleased to pour your Holy Spirit upon us.

As your Spirit came upon your prophets
and wise men of old, grant us your Spirit
of truth and understanding that we may
know your ways and walk in them.

As your Spirit came upon Christ at the Jordan,
grant us your Spirit of power and consecration
that we may enter into the ministry
and victory of your Son.

As your Spirit came upon your church in Jerusalem,
grant us your Spirit of grace and love that our lives
may more fully reflect your glory and that the world
might believe, to the honour of your name.

Through Jesus Christ our Lord.

Amen.

Lord of the winds and fires of earth

You are the breath and the fire
with which the word of God is spoken,

The wind on which the Gospel is borne
anywhere and to anyone in the world.

It is your work and the wonder of your inspiration
whenever people experience that Jesus lives.

That we follow him, that he becomes our way,
that men and women acknowledge that he is worth
all the trouble that this life can bring —
this is your enthusiasm and your power in us.

You are the life-giving Spirit that frees us,
dangerous and compelling
for those who cling to worldly goods and ties of blood.

You are both promise and uncertainty,
both poverty and grace.

We pray to you: give us life,
as you raised Jesus, our brother,
to life from the dead.

Make us fire of your fire,
light of your light,
as the Son of Man, Jesus,
is light of the eternal light in you
and God of God,
today and every day,
for ever and ever.
Amen.

In the stillness

Eternal God, show us deeply
how important it is
to care and not to care,
to let go and allow you to be Lord.

Lord, teach us the silence of humility,

The silence of wisdom,

The silence of love,

The silence that speaks without words,

The silence of faith.

Lord, teach us to silence
our own hearts and minds:

*That we may listen to the movement
of the Holy Spirit within us
and sense the depths
which are God.*

Amen.

Powers beyond our own

• I pray that the God of our Lord Jesus Christ,
the all-glorious Father, may give you
the spiritual powers of wisdom and perception,
by which there comes the knowledge of him.
I pray that the eyes of your heart
may be illumined, so that you may know
what is the hope to which he calls you,
what the wealth and glory
of the share he offers you among
his people in their heritage,
and how vast the resources of his power
open to us who trust in him. *

•• Holy Spirit of God,
giver of light and life,
impart to us:

Thoughts
higher than our own thoughts,

Prayers
better than our own prayers,

Powers
beyond our own powers,

That we may spend and be spent
in the ways of love and goodness,
after the image
of our Lord and Saviour
Jesus Christ.

Amen.

* Ephesians 1:17-19

The wind of the Spirit

- 'Listen to the wind, Nicodemus! Listen to the wind!
You can hear its sound — the night is full of it,
hark to it in the tops of the trees — but where it
has come from and where it is going no man knows.' *

•• Eternal God,
we praise you that your Spirit is like that —
invisible yet unmistakable,
impalpable yet full of power,

Able to do wonderful things for us
if only we will stand in its path
and turn our face to it
and open our life to its influence.

Almighty God,
we praise you that your Spirit is like that —
subject to the dictates and directions of no one,
no person, no church, no power.

Sometimes a judgment hurricane,
sometimes a gentle zephyr,
always your presence at work
creating, renewing, redeeming.

Sovereign God,
we praise you that your Spirit is like that —
mysterious and ceaseless,
elusive and intractable,

The very wind of heaven, scattering like leaves
the drabness and tedium of disillusioned lives,
melting the winter death of the soul,
cleaving open tombs that are closed.

*We praise you, O Lord, for the glory of Pentecost.
Come, Holy Spirit, come!*

* James S. Stewart

4

Welcoming

When we think back to the places
where we felt most at home, we
quickly see that it was where
our hosts gave us the precious
freedom to come and go on our own
terms and did not claim us for
their own needs. Only in a free
space can re-creation take place
and new life begin.

Henri Nouwen

For other prayers and readings
appropriate to the theme of the open
and welcoming church, and for
the occasion of welcoming a person
into the church community, see those
entitled:

Good news for celebration 23
Worship without pretence 24
Praise for the past and trust for
    the future 39
There is a new world 43
Risen and still with you 52
The goad of the promised future . 66
Recognizing the bonds 75
The rhythm of community 154

The scandal of grace 178
A surprising start 230
One Lord, one faith, one hope .. 234
Where the Spirit of the Lord is,
    there is freedom 236
The new commandment 251
More than we can measure or
    imagine 278

The open church

Father, you are not an absentee God.
You are constantly with us,
revealing new thoughts, doing new things,
to make us more aware of you.

In making yourself accessible to us,
you took a considerable risk.
By giving us the freedom to choose our own path,
you made yourself vulnerable
to disappointment and hostility,
as well as to love and obedience.

Your Son Jesus cared for all people.
Some listened to him and followed him,
others hated him;
but he was vulnerable and open to all —
Pharisee, prostitute, tax collector,
leper, widow, rich, poor.

Lord, we confess that in the name of piety
we have separated ourselves from the world
to which you have opened yourself.

Unlike Jesus who touched the leper,
hugged the demoniac,
accepted the adoration of the prostitute,
we seldom see the marginal people of our
society, nor do we touch them.

You have called us to be
the Body of Christ:

To reflect the openness of Christ to the world,
to the powerful and the powerless alike,
and to invite them to share his life with us.

Make us vulnerable
to the poor and needy.

Help us to see that being open to them
is not so much sharing our wealth
as sharing their poverty,
not so much sharing our power
as sharing their powerlessness,
not so much sharing our respectability
as sharing their stigma.

For we remember the grace of our Lord Jesus
who, though he was rich,
yet for our sake he became poor,
so that by his poverty we might become rich.

Help us to open our lives,
not our church buildings;
to open our homes,
not our church halls.

Help us to be the servant
not only of the beautiful, the capable,
the articulate and well educated,
but of the disabled and difficult,
the depressed and dispossessed.

Your Son Jesus was open to the hostility
of those whose vested interests
were threatened by him.

Give us the courage to be open
not only to praise and affirmation,
but also to receive rejection
from the ones who oppose your ways.

Most of all,
make us open to you.

Enter our lives
and fill us with the Spirit of Jesus,
so that our life together
may be a corporate reflection
of his presence in the world.

Amen.

A gift of grace

Together we are Christ's body,
but each of us is a different part of it.

Together we represent Christ to the world,
and in doing this each of us has a particular part to play.

It is by God's grace that we are members of this body.
*It is his grace that calls and equips us
in our particular ministry.*

(pause)

We thank you, Father, for your grace at work among us;
and particularly today we thank you for sending . . .
to join this community.

We recognize and accept him as a gift of your grace to us.

We know that you intend to speak to us
and shape us through him,
and we thank you for what he brings: his experiences,
his insights, his enthusiasm, his questions, his faith,
— his gift for ministry.

*We look forward to what he will spark off among us,
and what we will become because
you have brought us together.*

We thank you for all those influences
that have brought him to this moment.

*We pray that you will remind us continually
of the commitment we make to each other today.*

Lord, help us to encourage and stimulate,
to complement and exhort and support each other.

*Draw us together by the gifts of service
and ministry you plant in us.*

Deliver us from the temptation of taking each other
for granted or minimizing any person's contribution
to the whole ministry of your people.

*Keep before us the vision of wholeness which you
have given us in your Son,
and make us the people you want us to be.*

Through Jesus Christ our Lord.

Amen.

When appropriate, substitute the feminine pronoun for the masculine.

Children learn what they live

If children live with criticism,
they learn to condemn.

*If children live with hostility,
they learn to fight.*

If children live with ridicule,
they learn to be shy.

*If children live with shame,
they learn to feel guilty.*

If children live with tolerance,
they learn to be patient.

*If children live with encouragement,
they learn confidence.*

If children live with praise,
they learn to appreciate.

*If children live with fairness,
they learn justice.*

If children live with security,
they learn to have faith.

*If children live with approval,
they learn to like themselves.*

If children live with acceptance and friendship,
they learn to find love in the world.

This reading may be used with 'The blessing of a child'.

The blessing of a child

Pledge by Parents:

... and ..., in gratitude for the gift of ... you present
her in this way to her Lord. In dependence on God's grace,
will you endeavour, by example and teaching, to provide
her with a home of faith and love:

That she may know throughout her childhood and growth
into womanhood the warmth, hope, and freedom
of the Christian faith;

That she may welcome life's beauty, learn from its pain,
and share in its joys;

That her love for others may deepen with knowledge
and insight of every kind;

That she may discover what is the breadth and length
and height and depth of the love of God, and of his
Son Jesus Christ in whom he has made it known;

That her life may be open to the grace and purpose of God
and to the call of his Son, Jesus Christ our Lord?

Response: *We will.*

Pledge by Congregation:

And will you who belong to this church seek to be
a community in which ... can discover the meaning of
the Christian faith and stir into flame the gift
God has given her, whatever it be?

Response: *We will.*

Blessing:

The Lord bless you and watch over you,
the Lord make his face shine upon you
and be gracious to you,
the Lord look kindly on you and give you peace.

Amen.

When appropriate, substitute the masculine pronoun for the feminine,
and 'manhood' for 'womanhood'.

Commissioning

It is not revolutions and upheavals
that clear the road to new and better days
but revelations, lavishness and torments
of someone's soul, inspired and ablaze.

Boris Pasternak

For other prayers appropriate to the
theme of the call and commission of
the church, and for the occasion of
the commissioning of a person, see
those entitled:

The call of freedom has been
    sounded 21
Called to serve the cause of right 23
Mercy and freedom are his gifts . 26
To make your purpose our purpose 35
Maker of heaven and earth...... 37
Risen and still with you 52
Our call and commission 58
The community of grace 61

Our mission in the world 63
But not alone 147
Between already and not yet ... 170
The pledge of the Spirit 193
Breath of our life............... 279
Lord of the winds and fires of
    earth 280
Powers beyond our own 282

Induction of elders or deacons

Church Community and Minister:

There are different gifts,
but it is the same Spirit who gives them.

There are different ways of serving God,
but it is the same Lord who is served.

God works through different persons
in different ways,
*but it is the same God who achieves
his purpose through them all.*

Each one is given a gift by the Spirit,
to use it for the common good.

Together we are the Body of Christ,
and individually members of him.

Though we have different gifts,
together we are a ministry
of reconciliation
led by the risen Christ.

*It is therefore our prayer
that we may become a community
in which every member can discover
and stir into flame
the gift God has given,
whatever that gift may be.*

Minister to Elders or Deacons:

Recognizing the gifts you have to offer, we, ... ,
have set you apart as persons in whom we can
put our confidence and trust. We have called you to
be elders/deacons: to share in the leadership, pastoral over-
sight, and administration of our church. We do this
remembering the words of our Lord:

'You know that in the world the recognized
rulers lord it over their subjects, and
their great men make them feel the weight
of authority. That is not the way with you:
among you, whoever wants to be great must
be your servant, and whoever wants to be
first must be the willing slave of all.
For the Son of Man himself came not to be
served, but to serve, and to give his life
as a ransom for many.'

Do you welcome the work for which you have been chosen,
and will you, with God's help, serve this church with
energy, intelligence, imagination, and love:
make its welfare your concern,
the fellowship of the members to each other
your responsibility,
accept praise and not become proud,
criticism and not lose heart,
and finally, but not least,
be a friend to your fellow elders/deacons,
so that through your service together you may assist
our church in the continuing task of discovering the
mind of Christ, and therefore the ministry we have
to offer?

Response: *I do and I will.*

Induction of teachers or leaders

Church Community and Minister:

There are different gifts,
but it is the same Spirit who gives them.

There are different ways of serving God,
but it is the same Lord who is served.

God works through different persons
in different ways,
*but it is the same God who achieves
his purpose through them all.*

Each one is given a gift by the Spirit,
to use it for the common good.

Together we are the Body of Christ,
and individually members of him.

Though we have different gifts,
together we are a ministry
of reconciliation
led by the risen Christ.

*It is therefore our prayer
that we may become a community
in which every member can discover
and stir into flame
the gift God has given,
whatever that gift may be.*

Minister to Teachers or Leaders:

Recognizing the gifts
you have to offer,
this church has called you
to the ministry of teaching/leading
within our church family.

In the year that lies ahead will you,
as a disciple of Jesus Christ,
and with the support of those
who share your calling,
welcome your responsibilities;

commit yourself to a journey
of study, reflection, and discovery;
serve those who belong to your group
with intelligence and imagination,
sensitivity and love, sharing,
learning, and working together,
relying on God's grace
in all that you do?

Response: *I will.*   OR

Recognizing the gifts
you have to offer,
this church has called you
to lead and work with
young people.

In the year that lies ahead will you,
as a disciple of Jesus Christ,
and with the support of those
who share your calling,
welcome your responsibilities;

commit yourself to the preparation,
planning, reflection, and mastering
of skills your work will require;
serve those with whom you will journey
with intelligence and imagination,
sensitivity and love, sharing,
learning, and working together,
relying on God's grace
in all that you do?

Response: *I will.*

The commitment of the community

Lord, you have never waited for us to become perfect
before showing us the measure of your love,
or commissioning us to serve you in our world.

*We dare to believe you are always calling us to a
new venture; pointing us to new horizons in ministry,
and will never cease to do so.*

This is a task, Lord, we cannot do alone;
we need you as our guide,
and the love of each other.

*On this occasion we therefore claim the privilege
of committing ourselves anew to your service.*

With your help we will
bear one another's burdens,
and love our neighbour as ourself.

*We will accept disappointment and frustration,
opposition and rejection,
and not lose heart.*

We will love your world as you love it,
bring friendship into our work,
and courage into our politics.

*We will bring freshness into our homes,
excitement into our studies,
and adventure into our church.*

Create in us a clean heart, O God,
and renew a right spirit within us.
Stir into flame the gifts you have given,
and the faith to use them without reserve.

*As your disciples make us know the freedom
to move into the unknown and the untried,
to see the opportunities of the new day,
and to serve our present age with
compassion, imagination, and courage.*

*Lord, be with us until we have done our part
and share your joy. Amen.*

I lift my eyes to the hills Psalm 121

I lift my eyes to the hills:
where does my help come from?

Help comes to me from the Lord
who made heaven and earth.

*He will not allow your footsteps to slip,
he who watches over you will not sleep.*

*He who is the guardian of Israel
will neither slumber nor sleep.*

*The Lord himself is your keeper,
your defence at your right hand.*

*The sun shall not strike you by day,
nor the moon by night.*

*The Lord will keep you from all evil,
he will watch over your life.*

*He will be with you at your leaving
and in your coming back
from this time forward for evermore.*

This pilgrim psalm may be used as a prayer
of farewell for a missionary or person
moving to another community.

The person being farewelled asks the
question with which the psalm begins
and the congregation gives the response.

Go well, stay well

Lord, you have called . . . to another place,
another community, another task.

We are sad to see her go, but we recognize
that, just as she has been your gift to us,
so now she goes as a gift to another group
of your people.

We pray for each other now
as our once-parallel roads of pilgrimage diverge.

We thank you for all that we have done
or learnt or shared together.

We pray for . . . as she explores and clarifies
and puts into action
the call that takes her onward from here.

May she grow in your grace and in the knowledge
of your love, so that she may be a blessing to many.

We pray for the community to which she goes,
that they will value her, support her,
learn from her, and encourage her.

We pray for ourselves as we stay, that you will
keep us faithful to the vision we have shared,
and that you will show us what we should do,
how we should be, now that . . . is no longer with us.

As we part, we reaffirm that it has been your Spirit
who brought us together in the first place,
your Spirit who has enlivened our fellowship;

Your Spirit who goes with . . . ,
and your Spirit who stays with us;

Your Spirit who keeps us all together
in the world-wide family of your church.

Thanks be to God. Amen.

When appropriate, substitute the masculine pronoun for the feminine.

Parting

We shall not cease from exploration
and the end of all our exploring
will be to arrive where we started
and know the place for the first time.

T.S. Eliot

For other prayers and readings
appropriate to this section, see those
entitled:

Alpha and Omega 42
The meaning of providence...... 48
When the seas rage and mountains
    fall 49
God's everlasting kindness 50
Out of the depths 84

Things that make me sad 87
He is hidden 88
Shafts of trust 89
If I flew to the point of sunrise .. 99
Steps marking our way 119
Love's as warm as tears........ 335

Glimpses of a winding road

The Christian life is a journey with others;
we travel as a people, sharing our lives,
our experiences, our hopes and fears.

Lord, with joy and in hope we welcome new travellers
to share our lives, pledging ourselves to them,
wanting to learn from and with them,
offering our experiences to them, anticipating
the form which your grace will take in them,
so that we might become the people
you want us to be.

With gratitude and pain we farewell fellow travellers
who go in answer to your call to another congregation,
or who move ahead of us on the road through death.

Together we thank you for the gift of their lives
shared with us. Together we seek to support each other
in loss, to hear your word to us in bereavement,
to wait in expectation of the new beginnings
your Spirit will bring to our community.

Both in laying-hold and letting-go, we celebrate your
goodness to us, and affirm again the continuing
presence of your Spirit, blowing where you will,
forming and leading the life of your people.

Journey with us, sharing our triumphs and struggles,
and bring us safe into your eternal kingdom. Amen.

Strength to comfort 2 Corinthians 1:3-7

Blessed be the God and Father
of our Lord Jesus Christ,
a gentle Father
and the God of all consolation,

Who comforts us in all our sorrows,
so that we can offer others
the consolation that we ourselves
have received from God.

Indeed, as the sufferings of Christ
overflow to us,
so, through Christ,
does our consolation overflow.

When we are made to suffer,
it is for your consolation
and salvation.

When, instead, we are comforted,
it is to help us to bring you comfort,
and strength to face with fortitude
the same sufferings we now endure.

And our hope for you is firmly grounded;
for we know that if you share
our sufferings,
you will also share our consolations.

To your safe keeping

Gracious Lord,
in the face of death we gather together:

To celebrate the gift of . . .'s life
and to thank you for your word spoken in her.

*To open our hearts to you, offering
the brokenness of our feelings
and the fragments of our vision
for your understanding and healing.*

To hear again your word which comforts
and commissions us, and to express in
the solidarity and presence of this community
our love and concern for . . .'s family.

*To ask for the presence of your Spirit
as in love we commit her to your safe keeping,
and claim her in our hearts
as one of the cloud of witnesses
surrounding us on our pilgrimage.*

Amen.

When appropriate in this section, substitute the masculine pronoun
for the feminine, and vice versa.

Letting go

We thank you, our Father, for the life
of your servant . . . .

We thank you for the picture of your love
which has been given to us in his life;
for all you have given to us through him.

We still feel reluctant to let him go —
we need him so much. But we commit him
to you, knowing that he is safe with you.

We pray for his family. We pray, too,
for all of us who through his generous spirit
became part of his family.

We commit ourselves to you now, asking
that you will deal with the fears, anxieties,
old griefs awakened in us by . . .'s death.

Lord, free us to learn from his example,
to follow the way he has shown us,
to build on the foundation he has given,
and draw us together through your grace.

Give us the unshakeable knowledge
that there is nothing that can
separate us from your love
made visible in Jesus our Lord.

We thank you for the bonds
that hold us together and support us
even while we feel the pain of separation.
Help us to keep on supporting one another.

Give us your wisdom to grieve realistically,
with the hope of your new beginning in our
hearts; the courage to face a changed world
and to go out and live for you.

And may we know your grace, mercy,
and peace in our lives,
now and for evermore. Amen.

Valley of the shadow

Eternal God,
from whom we come and to whom we go,
we lift up our hearts to you for
courage and comfort in our need.
Death has come trampling into our life,
a sudden and savage enemy,
laying waste our hearts
and making desolate our minds.

We need now the consolation
only you can give.

O Father, we in this church family have lived
for a long time in the company of . . . .
We have accepted gratefully the gift she gave;
we felt her so much to be part
of what we might become tomorrow.

Her life spoke to us of your love,
and having her presence so deeply in our past
we took it for granted that she would be
with us in our journey into the future.
Now she is wrenched from us, and our hearts
are numb with the pain of love cut short.

O Father, you have said that when your children
cry out to you, you will hear and answer them;
you have said you will be close to them,
deliver them, and grant them eternal life.

Hear our cry, O Lord,
for we are your children.
Be near to us. Deliver us.
Let your eternal life live in us,
that we may be comforted
and find courage to go on.

But above all else we pray for . . .'s family.
This day brings to them a weight of sorrow
that is more than can be borne alone.

O Father, you have said that you care for
your own and deliver them in the midst
of the conflicts that plague them.

Hear our cry, O Lord,
for they are your own.
Bear them up in the midst
of the grief that afflicts them.

Heal their wounds. Deliver them from
a sense of hopelessness and give to them
your Holy Spirit that they may discover
the courage of hope and the love of life.

Assure them that, though we lose those
we love, none are lost to your love
which holds us in life and in death.

Grant, O Father, that the love we have
for . . . may not die, but be reborn
to deepen and sweeten the love we have
for each other and all people.

Make us more keenly aware of the value
and fragility of those you have given
to be our family and friends.

O God, draw us into closer relationship
with yourself and with each other
through this shared suffering.

Help us to lift our eyes above the dark
mystery of this earthly journey,
that we may see again more clearly
that eternal destiny which Christ has
prepared for those who love him.

And into your hands, O God,
we commend our lives,
through Jesus Christ our Lord.

Amen.

Your love is stronger than death

Our Father, God, we are in your hands;
we want to open ourselves to your perspective,
your grace and light.

And yet our feelings lock us into the present.
We offer them to you now:

Our shock at the news of . . .'s sudden death,
the numbness — it still doesn't seem real.

Our sadness at losing a friend,
the pain as our hearts ask: 'Why?'

Lord, these are some of the things we feel,
the questions that force their way
into our consciousness.

We offer them to you,
and ask you to comfort us
and lead us into truth.

We thank you that . . .'s trust was in you,
that faith was lived out in him,
that his life was grounded in your love.

Make us aware of that foundation now
and help us to ground our lives on you,
so that in our turmoil we will still
have you as our reference point,
in suffering we will know your presence:
know that it is in suffering that you
show yourself as God-with-us.

Meet us in this service,
through your Word spoken to us
and demonstrated in . . .'s life.

May we know healing in our grief,
peace in confusion,
your strength in our frailty.

Amen.

Footprints on the shore

The death of someone we love is the death of part of us.
No one else will ever call out from within us quite
the same responses, the same feelings or actions or ideas.
The death of someone we love is an ending
of one part of a story.

Lord, now as we look back over the life of . . .
as a completed whole we ask what we have received,
what we must appropriate and continue in our lives,
what must be laid to rest.

Our love for her reminds us that your bringing us
together in community gives us both support and pain.
Our being parted from her reminds us both of our
frailty and of your enduring love.

We thank you that our love for . . . draws us together
and gives us a new appreciation of each other,
and of the beauty and fragility of relationships
which mirror your grace and goodness to us.

Lord, time's tide may wash her footprints from the shore,
but not our love for her nor the influence of her life
upon our own, nor the ways in which they will ever be
a sign for us of those things which are eternal.

Amen.

5

Meditations for a Pilgrim People

The glory of self-realization and the misery of
self-estrangement alike arise from hopelessness in a
world of lost horizons. To disclose to our world
the horizon of the future of the crucified Christ
is the task of the Christian Church.

Jürgen Moltmann

Most of the meditations are presented in parts
which may be used separately or together.

A taste of sawdust and a thirst for truth

You can't put sawdust
in a meat pie
and expect it to be tasty.

Roy Miles

I

• People who are riddled with doubts
  tend to be dogmatists who are never wrong.

  John Powell

•• Until we recognize the right
  of the other person to be different,
  we are a long way from wisdom.

  Rex O'Brien

• If you disagree with me,
  you have something to give me,
  if you are sincere
  and seek the truth
  as best you may,
  honestly, with modest care,
  your thought is growth
  to mine, correction,
  you deepen my vision.

  Helder Camara

III

●● Error occurs whenever a half-truth
gets passed off as if it were the whole truth,
for then it becomes a perversion.

John Macquarrie

● The more readily we admit the possibility
of our own cherished convictions
being mixed with error,
the more vital and helpful
whatever is right in them will become;
and no error is so conclusively fatal
as the idea that God will not allow *us* to err,
though he has allowed all other men to do so.

John Ruskin

●● Also we confess, that we know but in part,
and that we are ignorant of many things
which we desire and seek to know.

And if any shall do us the friendly part,
and shew us from the Word of God that we see not,
we shall have cause to be thankful to God and to them.

But if any man shall impose on us anything
that we see not to be commended by our Lord Jesus Christ,
we should rather . . . die a thousand deaths, than to do
anything . . . against the light of our own consciences.

The 1646 Baptist Confession

III

•• Lord, forgive us:

When we fail to recognize the right
of the other person to be different.

*If we demand others to accept our ideas,
yet refuse even to consider theirs.*

When we want the thrill of discovery without
the search for truth and the torment of doubt.

*If we want things to be different,
but oppose any change.*

When we expect our church to be
what we ourselves refuse to give.

*If we impoverish our faith by believing
that the church exists only to meet our needs.*

Lord Jesus Christ, carpenter of Nazareth,
as we seek to learn from you
teach us that:

*We gain true understanding only as we share
in the trials and suffering of others;*

Yesterday's hurt may become today's understanding
woven into tomorrow's love;

*To have wisdom we must be open
to the unfamiliar and to the unsettling,
and willing to bear the pain that integrity brings.*

Lord,
may our love for each other increase more and more
and never stop improving our knowledge
and deepening our perception
so that we can always recognize what is best.*

Amen.

* Based on Paul's prayer in Philippians 1:9,10

Gossip

I

• Does anyone think he is a religious person?
If he does not control his tongue
his religion is worthless
and he deceives himself.

James 1:26

•• Gossip tells you more about the person
who tattles it
than about the person
whose life it pries into.

Berris Falla

• Think how small a flame
can set fire to a huge forest;
the tongue is a flame like that.

James 3:5

•• You will never be an inwardly
religious and devout person
unless you pass over in silence
the shortcomings of others,
and diligently examine your own weaknesses.

Thomas à Kempis

• If you forgive others their failings,
your heavenly Father will forgive you yours;
but if you do not forgive others, your
Father will not forgive your failings either.

Jesus
Matthew 6:14,15

•• O Church, Church,
   you that stone the prophets,
   that criticize those who dare to be different,
   that tear to pieces those who would serve you best;
   you that break reputations to pieces,
   who destroy growing souls with false kindness,
   who show one face to a man and another behind his back;
   who pour out the unkind gossip behind the hand:
   you judge without bringing to trial,
   you condemn without hearing the defence . . .

   In that hour alone shall you be open to receive my love,
   when you have forsaken judgment and found forgiving grace.

   Joan Brockelsby

• You, yes, you,
   why do you pass judgment on your brother?
   And you,
   why do you hold your brother in contempt?
   All of us will stand before God,
   to be judged by him.
   For the Scripture says,

   'As I live, says the Lord,
   everyone will kneel before me,
   and everyone confess that I am God.'

   So, you see, each of us
   will have to answer for himself.
   Far from passing judgment on each other, therefore,
   you should make up your mind never to be the cause
   of your brother tripping or falling.

   Paul of Tarsus
   Romans 14:10-13

III

●● It is true, Lord.

To appear righteous, we point a finger
at the faults of others.

To camouflage flaws in our own character,
we delight in the weaknesses of others.

To gain favour or promotion,
we assassinate someone's character.

To have something to say, we gossip
like crows cawing over scraps.

We criticize without thought
for the consequences.

We judge without understanding, and
condemn without knowing the circumstances.

Forgive us, and help us this very day
to make a new beginning.

● And now, my friends,
all that is true,
all that is noble,
all that is just and pure,
all that is lovable and gracious,
whatever is excellent and admirable —
fill all your thoughts with these things.

Paul of Tarsus
Philippians 4:8

Holiness

- I saw the Lord
  weeping
  with Aboriginal mothers
  around shanties
  and reservations
  where children learn little
  except early death
  or from their fathers
  the way of despair
  and toxic bitterness —
  weeping.

- Holy, holy, holy is the Lord of hosts;
  the whole earth is full of his glory.

- I saw the Lord
  gasping
  for breath in those churches
  wherever shallow worshippers
  mouth blessing on the hungry
  then drive home
  to overfills of protein
  and sport on the TV —
  gasping.

- Holy, holy, holy is the Lord of hosts;
  the whole earth is full of his glory.

- I saw the Lord
  hoping
  in students scanning open books
  roughly asking why
  why
  why
  searching deep into friendly eyes
  for seeds of truth
  worth living for
  and dying —
  hoping.

- Holy, holy, holy is the Lord of hosts;
  the whole earth is full of his glory.

- I saw the Lord
  agonizing
  through corridors and chambers
  of Canberra
  where hollow men
  salute expediency
  consult the opinion polls
  so that our future
  will be the past repeated
  spreading stench like the last —
  agonizing.

•• Holy, holy, holy is the Lord of hosts;
  the whole earth is full of his glory.

• I saw the Lord
  angry
  whenever church councils and committees
  tardily
  face agenda lifelessly
  with no fire in the gut
  no hope in the eye
  no readiness to lose all
  in the Kingdom which
  comes first —
  angry.

•• Holy, holy, holy is the Lord of hosts;
  the whole earth is full of his glory.

*O Lamb of God, who takes away the sins of the world,
have mercy upon us.
O Lamb of God, who takes away the sins of the world,
have mercy upon us.
O Lamb of God, who takes away the sins of the world,
grant us your peace.*

Bruce Prewer

Transformed nonconformist Romans 12:2

I

• Do not conform outwardly to the standards
of this world, but let God transform you
inwardly by a complete change of your mind.

Paul of Tarsus

•• Too many Christians
are not free
because they submit
to the domination
of other people's ideas.
They submit passively
to the opinions of the crowd.
For self-protection
they hide in the crowd,
and run along with the crowd.
They are afraid of the
aloneness,
the moral nakedness
which they would feel
apart from the crowd.

Thomas Merton

Break down, Lord Jesus, the barriers
of fear, timidity, and false humility
behind which we hide.
Speak to us from the cross and empty tomb
the word of pardon and freedom
that we may discover the will of God —
know what is good, and what it is
that God wants.

- But the Christian
  in whom Christ is risen
  dares
  to think and act differently
  from the crowd.
  He has ideas of his own,
  not because he is arrogant,
  but because he has the humility
  to stand alone
  and pay attention to the purpose
  and the grace of God,
  which are often quite contrary
  to the purposes and the plans
  of the established
  human power structure.

  Thomas Merton

II

- Neither Jesus who calls us to follow him,
  nor Paul his apostle, leave us any choice:
  whoso would be a Christian
  must also be a nonconformist.
  Any Christian who blindly accepts
  the opinions of the majority
  and in fear and timidity follows a path
  of expediency and social approval
  is a mental and spiritual slave.

  Martin Luther King

●● Lord Jesus Christ, we confess that, instead
  of responding to the demands of the Gospel,
  we have often marched to the drumbeat
  of conformity and respectability.

  With concern, yet unease, we confess
  to the church's tragic tendency
  to conform, crystallize, conserve, and even bless
  the pattern of majority opinion.

With deep shame we confess
to the church's sanction
of slavery, racial discrimination, poverty,
war, and economic exploitation.

With sorrow we admit that we,
whom you have called to be your people,
have hearkened more to the authority of the world
than to the authority of our Father, God.

III

• They are slaves who fear to speak
for the fallen and the weak;
they are slaves who will not choose
hatred, scoffing, and abuse,
rather than in silence shrink
from the truth they needs must think;
they are slaves who dare not be
in the right with two or three.

James Russell Lowell

•• But only through an inner spiritual transformation
do we gain the strength to fight vigorously
the evils of the world
in a humble and loving spirit.
The transformed nonconformist, moreover,
never yields to the passive sort of patience
which is an excuse to do nothing.
And this very transformation saves him
from speaking irresponsible words
which estrange without reconciling,
and from making hasty judgments which are blind
to the necessity of social progress.
He recognizes
that social change will not come overnight,
yet he works
as though it is an imminent possibility.

Martin Luther King

Lord, give us
the serenity to accept
  what cannot be changed;
the courage to change
  what ought to be changed;
and the wisdom to distinguish
  the one from the other.

Reinhold Niebuhr

IV

• Honesty compels me to admit that transformed nonconformity,
which is always costly and never altogether comfortable,
may mean walking through the valley
of the shadow of suffering, losing a job,
or having a six-year-old daughter ask,
'Daddy, why do you have to go to jail so much?'
But we are gravely mistaken to think
that Christianity protects us
from the pain and agony of mortal existence.
Christianity has always insisted
that the cross we bear
precedes the crown we wear.

Martin Luther King

Come, Lord Jesus, come,
and teach us again that to be your disciples
we must take up our cross,
with all its difficulties and agonizing
and tragedy-packed content,
and carry it until that very cross
leaves its marks upon us and redeems us
to that more excellent way
which comes only through suffering.

The second and fourth prayers are
derived from Martin Luther King's
sermon 'Transformed Nonconformist'

Fortitude

- But the big courage is the cold-blooded kind, the kind
  that never lets go even when you're feeling empty inside,
  and your blood's thin, and there's no kind of fun or profit
  to be had, and the trouble's not over in an hour or two,
  but lasts for months and years. One of the men here
  was speaking about that kind, and he called it 'Fortitude'.
  I reckon fortitude's the biggest thing a man can have —
  just to go on enduring when there's no guts or heart
  left in you. Billy had it when he trekked solitary
  from Garungoze to the Limpopo with fever and a broken arm
  just to show the Portugooses that he wouldn't be downed by
  them. But the head man at the job was the Apostle Paul.

- This is Paul speaking: Let us exult in the hope
  of the divine splendour that is to be ours.
  More than this: let us exult even in our
  present sufferings, because we know that suffering
  trains us to endure, and endurance brings proof
  that we have stood the test, and this proof
  is the ground of hope. Such a hope is no mockery,
  because God's love has flooded our inmost heart
  through the Holy Spirit he has given us.

- As God's servants, we try to recommend ourselves
  in all circumstances by our steadfast endurance:
  in hardships and dire straits; flogged, imprisoned,
  mobbed; overworked, sleepless, starving. We recommend
  ourselves by the innocence of our behaviour,
  our grasp of truth, our patience and kindliness;
  with gifts of the Holy Spirit, by sincere love,
  by declaring the truth, by the power of God.
  We wield the weapons of righteousness in right hand
  and left. Honour and dishonour, praise and blame,
  are alike our lot: we are the impostors who speak
  the truth, the unknown men whom all men know;
  dying, we still live on; disciplined by suffering,
  we are not done to death; in our sorrows
  we have always cause for joy; poor ourselves,
  we bring wealth to many; penniless, we own the world.

•• God, our Father,
   this makes our lives and religion
   seem like wood, hay, and stubble;
   we are humbled, but also take heart.

   *We give you thanks for Paul of Tarsus,
   and all those like him, whose fortitude,
   love, and vision of your kingdom
   light the fires of courage and faith
   in our own hearts:*

   For Jeremiah and Stephen,
   Martin Luther and Felix Manz,*
   Dietrich Bonhoeffer and Martin Luther King,
   Helder Camara and Mother Teresa.

• And now with them and all those
   like them, known and unknown to us,
   we make this prayer of Paul,
   your apostle, our own:

   *My one hope and trust is that
   I shall never have to admit defeat,
   but that now as always I shall
   have courage, so that with my whole
   being I shall bring honour to Christ,
   whether by my life or by my death.*

   Amen.

*Felix Manz was the first Zurich
 Anabaptist martyr.
 He was drowned
 in the River Limmat
 on January 25, 1527.

Sources:
John Buchan's Mr. Standfast;
Romans 5:2-5;
2 Corinthians 6:4-10;
Philippians 1:20.

Happiness is . . .

I

- Happiness is . . .
- What is happiness?

- 'Happiness is not something to be searched for;
  still less something you can make;
  it is something you can only receive,
  and become.'

- Psalm 1 says,
  'Happy are those
  who reject the advice of evil men,
  who do not follow the example of sinners
  or join those who have no use for God.
  Instead, they find joy obeying
  the law of the Lord,
  and they study it day and night.'

- Happiness is for those who will
  deliberately turn from evil
  and seek God.
  They will be happy
  because they will find him.

  *Happiness is the sheer delight
  of walking in the light of God's presence.*

II

- Happiness is . . .
- What is happiness?

- Jesus said happiness is poverty,
  but most of us spend our lives
  slaving to avoid it.
  Poverty is happiness:
  God is on the side of the poor;
  he chooses to give the kingdom
  to the powerless.

- Those who are rich, who take more
  than their fair share of this world's goods,
  who look to things and forget people,
  will experience the judgment of God.

True happiness is for the poor in spirit:
not only those who have little money,
but those who know they need
to depend on God.

*Happiness is the joyous freedom of discovering
the emptiness of possessions and the richness of God.*

III

- Happiness is . . .
- • What is happiness?

- Jesus said happiness is for the grief-stricken.
  Surely those who mourn the loss of a loved one
  cannot be called happy;
  those who mourn the misery of the poor
  and oppressed are not happy;
  those who grieve the genocide
  of Australian Aborigines and American Indians,
  who mourn the death of a race and its culture
  cannot be called happy!

- • Jesus said those who mourn will be comforted.
  Sorrows and difficulties offer the opportunity
  to discover hidden strengths and weaknesses.
  Grief can reveal our need
  of someone stronger than ourselves.
  Real happiness is for those
  who through their pain discover
  themselves and the world;
  who find their strength and consolation
  in the God who shares their grief.

*Happiness is the surprising delight that is certain
of God's ultimate purpose for his creation.*

IV

- Happiness is . . .
- • What is happiness?

- Jesus said meek people are happy.
  They know how to be angry at the right time
  at injustice, cruelty, prejudice.
  They have allowed God to control
  impulses and passions.
  They are humble enough to be aware
  of their own ignorance and weakness.

- • They have learnt that love
  is the power that cannot be corrupted;
  that the desire to dominate
  must be turned into the energy that serves.
  They have learnt to allow God
  to set the pace of daily life.

  *Happiness is the absolute confidence that God
  gives strength to the meek and powerless.*

V

- Happiness . . .
- • What is happiness?

- Jesus said happy are those
  who are hungry and thirsty
  to know and do that which is right.
  They will be truly fed.
  We know the common experience
  of ordinary hunger and thirst.
  Many in our world know the hunger
  and thirst that lead to death.

●● Jesus meant this degree of hunger and thirst:
a desperate craving, an intense longing
for God's purposes to be established on earth.
Those who yearn with God for the fulfilment
of his justice will be satisfied.

*Happiness is the confident hope of watching and
working for the certain coming of his kingdom.*

VI

● Happiness is . . .
●● What is happiness?

● Jesus said merciful people are happy.
To show mercy is to show strength.
Merciful people recognize the needs
and weaknesses of others,
because they are aware of the needs
and weaknesses they experience in themselves.

●● They are able to feel with others
and not simply for them.
Their acts of kindness
arise from understanding,
and not just from the need
to relieve their own discomfort.
They are able to give mercy
because they have accepted
God's mercy already.

*Happiness is the ultimate joy of sharing
with the world the mercy of the compassionate God.*

VII

- Happiness is . . .
- What is happiness?

- Jesus said the people
  who are pure in heart are happy.
  Purity of heart is much more than
  innocent unawareness of the evil
  that abounds.
  The pure in heart are those
  who positively love
  that which is good.
  Their lives focus on
      love,
        joy,
          peace,
            beauty,
              justice,
                graciousness,
                  and honour.

- They are the people who will see God,
  for they will have their vision trained.

  *Happiness is the amazing joy of those who work
  in poverty of spirit, in meekness of heart,
  and with singleness of purpose.*

VIII

- Happiness is . . .
- What is happiness?

- Jesus said the people who make peace are happy.
  These are the ones who actively foster
  good relationships between people and nations.
  They deliberately, thoughtfully,
  take positive steps to bring harmony
  in place of conflict.

•• They know that, through Jesus Christ,
   God's peace is available in human affairs.
   Peacemakers know that peace is more
   than the absence of conflict.
   True peace reconciles opposites,
   creating a new and growing unity.
   True peacemakers are God-like people,
   for God desires and works for peace.

   *Happiness is the wholeness that comes
   from working with God for peace.*

IX

• Happiness is . . .
•• What is happiness?

• Jesus said happiness belongs to those
   who suffer because they follow him.
   Much of our suffering is the result
   of our own folly or mistakes;
   some is the inevitable result
   of being human.

•• Few of us know the privilege of suffering
   solely because we are disciples.
   Let us pray for all who do.
   Persecution for the faith provides
   an opportunity to sort out real loyalties.
   It links us with those
   who have suffered through the ages.
   It brings us closer companionship
   with the Christ who also suffered.

   *Happiness is the fortitude, the resolute obedience,
   forged from a faith worth suffering for.*

X

- Happiness is . . .
- What is happiness?

- Jesus said happiness is the reward of those
  who can believe even before they are given proof.
  Most of us want things proved before we can believe.
  Even Thomas wanted to touch Jesus
  to be sure he had risen.

- For those who believe like this,
  believing is seeing, believing is touching.
  Jesus said happiness is for those
  who can stake their lives
  on his death and resurrection,
  his gift of life eternal,
  without having tangible proof.

*Happiness is the eternal bliss of those whose faith
enables them to see the unseen realities.*

Adele Davies

Love's as warm as tears

• If I speak in the tongues of men and of angels,
but have not love,

I am no more than a noisy gong
or a clanging cymbal.

If I have the gift of prophecy
and can fathom all mysteries and all knowledge,
if I have faith that can move mountains,
but have not love,

I am nothing.

If I give away everything I have
or even give my body to be burnt,
but have not love,

I gain nothing.

Love is patient;
love is kind and envies no one.

Love is never boastful,
nor conceited, nor rude.

Love is never selfish,
nor quick to take offence.

Love keeps no score of wrongs,
does not gloat over other people's sins,
but delights in the truth.

There is nothing love cannot face;
there is no limit to its faith,
its hope, and its endurance.

Love will never come to an end.

Are there prophets? Their work will be over.
Are there tongues of ecstasy? They will cease.
Is there knowledge? It will vanish away.

For our knowledge is imperfect,
and our prophecy is imperfect;
but, when perfection comes,
all imperfect things will disappear.

When I was a child, I talked like a child,
I thought like a child, I reasoned like a child;
when I became a man, I gave up childish ways.

What we can see now is like a dim reflection in a mirror,
but then we shall see face to face.

My knowledge now is partial;
then it will be whole —
like God's knowledge of me.

In a word, there are three things
that last for ever: faith, hope, and love;
but the greatest of them all is love.

•• Love's as warm as tears,
love is tears:
pressure within the brain,
tension at the throat,
deluge, weeks of rain,
haystacks afloat,
featureless seas between
hedges, where once was green.

Love's as fierce as fire,
love is fire:
all sorts — infernal heat
clinkered with greed and pride,
lyric desires, sharp-sweet,
laughing, even when denied
and that empyreal flame
whence all loves came.

Love's as fresh as spring,
love is spring:
bird-song hung in the air,
cool smells in a wood,
whispering 'Dare! Dare!'
to sap, to blood,
telling 'Ease, safety, rest,
are good; not best'.

Love's as hard as nails,
love is nails:
blunt, thick, hammered through
the medial nerves of One
who, having made us, knew
the thing He had done,
seeing (with all that is)
our cross, and His.

Sources:
1 Corinthians 13;
poem by C.S. Lewis

337

Step into joy

A meditation in four parts, on being sensitive
to the world, to others, to ourselves
and to God.

I

- Life means:
  give and take
  making mistakes
  being disappointed
  letting yourself down
  need for courage
  inevitability of death
  growth and pain
  insecurity and anxiety
  learning to cope
  leaning on others
  standing on your own feet
  winning happiness
  self-discipline and joy
  being sensitive.

- ● You say, 'Life is being sensitive'.
  Isn't sensitivity a sign of weakness?

- A man sits in front of a bad television program
  and does not know that he is bored;
  he learns of the danger of nuclear holocaust
  and does not feel fear;
  he joins the rat race of commerce —
  where personal worth is measured
  in terms of market values —
  and is not aware of his anxiety.
  What we confront now is the possibility
  that man is dead,
  transformed into a thing,
  a producer, a consumer,
  and idolator of other things.

  Eric Fromm

Sensitivity, a sign of weakness?

But can we live without responding
to the world around us,
to other people,
to the depths within us,
to God?

Are we sensitive to the world around us?

God help me
to feel wonder —
in a leaf
in a ray of sun
in a snowfall.
To laugh and cry
with somebody else
or all by myself.
To let gaiety into my life
and to show someone else how.
To take a friend's hand
for no special reason.
To value the small things
but to want to do great things.
To believe what your Son said about
becoming like little children.
May I be at home in your kingdom.

••• Here is a day, a golden day,
be lavish as you spend it;
new and bright shining after rain,
immaculate with promise, yours for the taking,
rare with fine gold, it will not come again.

Spend it in ecstasy of worship,
sailing the wind, with sunshine, sea, and rain;
by great hills, gorse and heather mantled,
patterned with racing cloud, then sun again.

Pour out with boldness, walk in singleness and splendour,
let flower, mountain, friend an altar be,
for every moment holds a joy for your beholding,
each tear of dew a light that only you can see.

This is a day for you prepared,
be reckless as you spend it,
let no exalted moment pass you by,
for every fallen leaf bears your appointed pattern
and lo, not one, but seven rainbows span the sky.

Joan Brockelsby

Morning has broken

Morning has broken
Like the first morning,
Blackbird has spoken
Like the first bird.
    Praise for the singing!
    Praise for the morning!
    Praise for them, springing
Fresh from the Word!

Sweet the rain's new fall
Sunlit from heaven,
Like the first dewfall
On the first grass.
    Praise for the sweetness
    Of the wet garden,
    Sprung in completeness
Where his feet pass.

Mine is the sunlight!
Mine is the morning!
Born of the one light
Eden saw play!
    Praise with elation,
    Praise every morning,
    God's re-creation
Of the new day!

Eleanor Farjeon

II

• We learn

> to trust, by being trusted;
> to hope, by learning to believe;
> to be faithful, by the fidelity of others toward us;
> to be moderate, by the moderation of others;
> to excel, by the excellence of others.

Are we sensitive to others?

•• Does a teacher show his love for his students
by giving them the answers to their problems
for fear they'll make a mistake?

Does a mother show her love for her baby
by refusing to teach him to walk for fear he'll fall?

Does a father show his love for his son
by forbidding him to go out for fear he'll get into trouble?

Michel Quoist

• We learn

> to give, by receiving;
> to love, by being loved;
> to forgive, by being forgiven;
> to tolerate, by being tolerated;
> to accept, by being accepted.

> Lucy: Merry Christmas, Charlie Brown!
> At this time of year I think we should put
> aside all our differences, and try to be kind.

> Charlie Why does it have to be for just this time of year . . .?
> Brown: Why can't it be all year round?

> Lucy: What are you, some kind of fanatic
> or something?

●●● I'm hurting inside;
     hurting because we are treated like migrants
         in our own country;
     hurting because some white people don't
         understand how we feel;
     hurting because we aren't treated
         as human beings.

     It hurts
     when you call me an Abo;
     when we are looked down upon;
     when we watch our children being
         treated like dirt.
     It hurts when you don't understand.

     Won't you help us bridge the gap between
         your people and ours?
     We have so much to give each other
         if only given a chance.
     Won't you accept us as we are —
         people with feelings the same as you?
     Won't you try to understand how we
         feel about our culture, our land —
         try to understand our needs?
     Won't you try to understand
         the hurt,
             the heart-ache,
                 the discouragement,
                     the disappointment?

Daphne Lowe
Victoria, 1981

●● In spite of our deep-seated craving for love,
     almost everything else is considered
     to be more important than love:
     success, money, power —
     almost all our energy is used in learning
     how to achieve these aims, and almost none
     in learning how to love.

Eric Fromm

                         (pause)

                         343

- What is good has been explained to you:
  only this,
    to act justly,
      to love tenderly,
        and to walk humbly with your God.

Micah

●● Always treat others as you would like them
  to treat you: that is the Law and the Prophets.

Jesus

- There should be no competition among you, no conceit.
  Always consider the other person to be better than yourself
  so that nobody thinks of his own interests first
  but everybody thinks of other people's interests instead.
  In your minds you must be the same as Christ Jesus.

Paul of Tarsus

●● The hungry person needs bread,
  and the homeless needs a roof;
  the dispossessed needs justice,
  and the lonely needs friendship.
  The undisciplined needs order,
  and the slave needs freedom.
  To allow the hungry person to remain hungry
  would be a blasphemy against God
  and one's neighbour, for what is nearest to God
  is precisely the need of one's neighbour.

Dietrich Bonhoeffer

●●● I give you a new commandment:
  love one another; just as I have loved you,
  you must also love one another.

Jesus

344

Lord, let me see

1.
Lord, let me see, see more and more,
See the beauty of a person, not the colour of his skin,
See the faces of the homeless with no one to take them in,
See discouragement because she'll never win,
See the face of our Lord in the pain.
Lord, let me see.

2.
Lord, let me hear, hear more and more,
Hear the sounds of great rejoicing, hear a person barely sigh,
Hear the ring of truth, and hollowness of those who live a lie,
Hear the wail of starving people who will die,
Hear the voice of our Lord in the cry.
Lord, let me hear.

3.
Lord, let me care, care more and more,
Care for those who feel the loneliness, for those who have no say,
Care for friends who have no job and find it hard to face the day,
Care for those with whom we sing and work and pray,
And in care Jesus Christ will be found.
Lord, let me care.

4.
Lord, let me learn, learn more and more,
Learn that what I know is just a speck of what there is to know,
Learn from listening to my brother when I'd rather speak and go,
Learn that as we live in faith and trust we grow,
Learn to see, hear, and care, with our Lord.
Lord, let me learn.

5.
Lord, let me love, love more and more,
Love the loveless and the fragile, help them be what they can be,
Love the way that I would like them to be looking after me,
For to know you is to love them and be free,
And in love Jesus Christ will be found.
Lord, let me love.

Words and music: Ross Langmead

III

- Look at the birds flying around:
  they do not plant seeds,
  gather a harvest, and put it in barns;
  your Father in heaven takes care of them!
  Aren't you worth much more than birds?
  Which one of you can live a few more years
  by worrying about it?

And why worry about clothes?
Look how the wild flowers grow:
they do not work or make clothes for themselves.
But I tell you that not even Solomon,
as rich as he was, had clothes
as beautiful as one of these flowers.
It is God who clothes the wild grass —
grass that is here today, gone tomorrow,
burnt up in the oven.
Won't he be all the more sure to clothe you?

Jesus

Are we sensitive to ourselves?

Father, help me to know myself:
what I am and what I can become.
Enable me to see the good in myself
and rejoice in it,
to see flaws and change them.
Teach me to live with myself,
to accept myself.
Remind me
that becoming what you want me to be
is more like cultivating a garden
than chopping down a forest.

•• Rivers can only continue their motion when
waters flows along their banks creating
life within their essence.

I can only give what awareness I have
inside me.
You can only receive that which you are aware
is your need.

We are rivers unto one another:
this time called life was made to share.

Walter Rinder

••• What sort of Christian then
does this present time call for?
Not one who is
fear-ridden and insecure,
inhibited and ossified,
prim and plaintive,
fanatical and filled with resentment,
but a Christian who is
courageous and self-reliant,
big in ideas and in heart,
dynamic and vital,
open and joyful.
All this is given by Christian freedom:
generosity and naturalness,
humour, individuality,
strength, self-reliance,
courage to think and to decide,
hope and be joyful.

Hans Küng

Spirit, be our Spirit

With movement and feeling

Gregory Norbet.

349

Spirit, be our Spirit
in this time of searching for new life.
Open inner spaces
with the fullness of your love.
**Spirit, let us now be and for ever
transformed for all humanity.**

Movement of your presence
heals and deepens our hope to freely live.
Gift of heart where truth springs
from the goodness that you've sown:

Into desert silence,
there to listen and be with open heart,
you shall lead us, thirsting;
and we turn from our fears:
forgiving love.

Words and Music: Gregory Norbet

IV

- One day I was stopped by Sunday-school Teacher.
Sunday-school Teacher asked me, no, told me, to
instruct Anna to behave herself in the class. I
asked what it was that Anna had done or had not
done and was told: one, that Anna interrupted,
two, that Anna contradicted, and three, that Anna
used bad language. Anna could, I admit, use a
pretty good cuss-word at times and I tried to
explain to Sunday-school Teacher that, although
Anna sometimes used language badly, she never
in fact used the language of badness. My arrow
missed the target completely. I could well imagine
that Anna had interrupted her and also that she
had contradicted her, but she wouldn't tell me
the circumstances of this episode. That evening
I spoke to Anna on the subject. I told her that
I had met Sunday-school Teacher and told her
what had been said.
'Not going to no Sunday school no more.'
'Why not?'
' 'Cos she don't teach you nuffink about Mister
God.'
'Perhaps you don't listen properly.'
'I do, and she don't say nuffink.'
'You mean to say you don't learn anything?'
'Sometimes.'
'Oh, that's good. What do you learn?'
'Sunday-school Teacher is frightened.'
'What makes you say that sort of thing; how do
you know that she's frightened?'
'Well, she won't let Mister God get bigger.'

Fynn, *Mister God this is Anna*

(pause)

•• The world will never be vast enough,
nor will humanity ever be strong enough,
to be worthy of him who created
them and incarnated himself in them.

Pierre Teilhard de Chardin

••• O Lord, our Lord,
how great your name throughout the earth!

Above the heavens is your majesty chanted
by the mouths of children, babes in arms.
You set your stronghold firm against your foes
to subdue enemies and rebels.

I look at your heavens, made by your fingers,
at the moon and stars you set in place —
what is man that you should spare a thought for him,
the son of man that you should care for him?

Yet you have made him little less than a god,
you have crowned him with glory and splendour,
made him lord over the works of your hands,
set all things under his feet,

Sheep and oxen, all these,
yes, wild animals, too,
birds in the air, fish in the sea
travelling the paths of the ocean.

O Lord, our Lord,
how great your name throughout the earth!

- Creator God,
  you are familiar with the things we care about,
  you know our strengths and weaknesses,
  you share our joy and pain,
  and our hearts are tender in the thought of you.

  *May nothing ever succeed in wooing us away
  from you, and may the call of Jesus your Son
  never fail to find access to our hearts.*

  May we never be so devoted to the mirage of
  the world, to the creature instead of the Creator,
  that we lose sight of your everlasting love.

  *God our Saviour,
  be the dawn for which we wait and look,
  the hope by which we live,
  the joy for which we long;
  be our freedom, Lord, now and for ever.*

  Amen.

                              (pause)

●● Follow, poet, follow right
   to the bottom of the night.
   With your unconstraining voice
   still persuade us to rejoice;

   With the farming of a verse
   make a vineyard of the curse,
   sing of human unsuccess
   in a rapture of distress;

   In the desert of the heart
   let the healing fountain start,
   in the prison of his days
   teach the free man how to praise.

   W.H. Auden

Search for the infant born

Paul Carter

Search for the infant born in a stable,
　　Search where it's humble, search where it's poor.
Man's search for God finds rest in a stable,
　　There in the smell and warmth of the straw.
See the infant, what a wonder!
　　See the mother's tender care.
Cow and ass stand close together,
　　While their bodies warm the air.

Search for the man who travels the country,
　　Feeding the hungry, healing the blind.
Man's search for God finds rest in the needy,
　　There with the outcasts of every kind.
There the word of love is spoken,
　　There the truth of God made clear,
In the country, up on the hillside,
　　People in thousands jostle to hear.

Search for the man who hangs on a gallows,
　　Nailed there by hatred, nailed there by fear.
Man's search for God finds rest at the gallows,
　　There at the cross the answer is near.
Hear the mocking, hear the scorning,
　　See the blood and feel the pain.
On the hilltop, nailed to the gallows,
　　Love meets rejection, all seems in vain.

Search for the man who's risen for ever,
　　Out on the highway, down by the shore.
Man's search for God finds truth in his spirit,
　　Still with the needy, still with the poor.
Where there's hunger, where there's hatred,
　　Where injustice, where there's pain,
Out of the stable, out of the country,
　　Down from the gallows, Jesus does reign.

Roy Ward

Footnote to all prayers

He whom I bow to only knows to whom I bow
when I attempt the ineffable Name, murmuring *Thou*,
and dream of Pheidian fancies and embrace in heart
symbols (I know) which cannot be the thing Thou art.
Thus always, taken at their word, all prayers blaspheme
worshipping with frail images a folk-lore dream,
and all men in their praying, self-deceived, address
the coinage of their own unquiet thoughts, unless
Thou in magnetic mercy to Thyself divert
our arrows, aimed unskilfully, beyond desert;
all men are idolators, crying unheard
to a deaf idol, if Thou take them at their word.

Take not, O Lord, our literal sense. Lord, in Thy great,
unbroken speech our limping metaphor translate.

C.S. Lewis

INDEXES

PRAYERS ESPECIALLY SUITABLE FOR CHILDREN

Belonging 135
Every part of our life 130
Fun times 76
God gives 134
Grass by the roadside 78
Limb and mind in harmony 133
Many lovely things 134
Sharing 134
Things that make me sad 87

TITLES: ALPHABETICAL LISTING

The references to authors and sources are intended only as a
guide to the following index where details, including
secondary sources, are given in full.

A gift of grace (Bruce Rumbold) 290
A letter not written with ink (Terry Falla) 125
A litany for the Lucky Country (Anonymous) 142
A people on trial (Terry Falla) 94
A plea for God's forgiveness (Micah 7:18-20) 98
A prayer of Ignatius Loyola 118
A surprising start (Athol Gill) 230
A taste of sawdust and a thirst for truth (Terry Falla) 314
A world in which faith comes hard (Terry Falla) 144
Acclaim with joy the depths of his love (Terry Falla) 38
Against the wind (Terry Falla) 156
Alive! (Terry Falla) 68
Alpha and Omega (Terry Falla) 42
Attune us to your silence (Huub Oosterhuis) 34

Because you believe in us (David Griffiths) 32
Belonging (Terry Falla) 135
Between already and not yet (Terry Falla) 170
Beyond all pretence (Caryl Micklem, editor) 103
Beyond what the silent stars tell (Terry Falla) 224
Blindness (Annals) 112
Bread with laughter (Brian Frost) 162
Breath of our life (Athol Gill) 279
Broken bones may joy (Psalm 51) 85
Brought together to break bread (An Order for Holy
    Communion) 184
But not alone (Let's Worship) 147

Called to serve the cause of right (Isaiah 42:5-7) 23
Children learn what they live (Anonymous) 291
Choices (Terry Falla) 240
Christmastide profiles (Terry Falla) 214
Come away (Anonymous) 35
Come, Lord (Helder Camara) 174
Confessions at the empty tomb (Norman C. Habel) 272
Cosmic hymn of praise (Psalm 148) 82
Counterfeit? (Ronald N. Ham) 156

Courage to change (Terry Falla) 132
Crucified risen one! (Leader's Guide to *Move Man!*) 275

Dawn for our darkness (Luke 1:68-79) 204
Delivered to death for our misdeeds (Leader's Guide
   to *Move Man!*) 270
Do this, remembering me (*An Order for Holy
   Communion*) 182
Doing the truth (Terry Falla) 248
Dreams for celebration (Norman C. Habel) 194

Emmanuel (Terry Falla) 210
Enough! (Terry Falla) 120
Eternal God and mortal man (Leslie F. Brandt) 96
Every part of our life (Terry Falla, Judith Jones and
   Rex O'Brien) 130

Failed (*Let's Worship*) 114
Father, forgive (Coventry Cathedral Pamphlets) 105
Find your love (Michelle Stewart) 154
Footnote to all prayers (C.S. Lewis) 356
Footprints on the shore (Bruce Rumbold) 309
For our city and ourselves (David Griffiths) 140
Forbid! (John Baillie) 138
Forgiveness (Graeme Griffin) 250
Forsaken? (Bruce Prewer) 269
Fortitude (Terry Falla) 326
Free to forget our pride (Caryl Micklem, editor) 107
Fun times (Daniel, Jeremy, Matthew and Terry Falla) 76

Given for the life of the world (*An Order for
   Holy Communion*) 180
Glimpses of a winding road (Bruce Rumbold) 302
Gloria in excelsis (ICET) 40
Go well, stay well (Bruce Rumbold) 300
Go with us, Lord (Caryl Micklem, editor) 137
God gives (Simon Narkeiwicz) 134
God saw all that he had made (Terry Falla) 128
God's everlasting kindness (Psalm 103) 50
Good Friday (Bruce Prewer) 268
Good news for celebration (Anonymous) 23
Gossip (Terry Falla) 317
Granting of forgiveness (House of the Gentle Bunyip) 177
Grass by the roadside (Rex O'Brien) 78

Hallelujah for the Christ-child! (Graeme Garrett) 216
Happiness is . . . (Adele Davies) 328
He is hidden (Terry Falla) 88
He is one of us (Karl Barth) 205
Healings from the empty tomb (Norman C. Habel) 274
Here and now (Alan Gaunt) 20
Holiness (Bruce Prewer) 320

I have betrayed (Leader's Guide to *Move Man!*) 98
I have called you by name (Psalm 100) 39
I lift my eyes to the hills (Psalm 121) 299
If I flew to the point of sunrise (Psalm 139) 99
In all things be our strength (*The Worshipbook*) 124
In awe and welcome stand (Psalm 8) 81
In the stillness (Pauline Webb, editor) 281
Induction of elders or deacons (Terry Falla) 294
Induction of teachers or leaders (Terry Falla) 296

Jesus (Anonymous) 100
Jesus our Lord (*Praise in All Our Days*) 260
Joy comes in the morning (Psalm 30) 71
Just as we are (Terry Falla) 181

Let the winds of the Spirit (Terry Falla) 36
Letting go (Bruce Rumbold) 305
Liberty to the oppressed (Terry Falla) 166
Life can begin again (Alan Wade) 46
Light of the world (Terry Falla) 226
Limb and mind in harmony (David Griffiths and
    Rex O'Brien) 133
Longing for tomorrow and losing today (Jo Carr and
    Imogene Sorley) 90
Lord of the storm (Psalm 29) 79
Lord of the winds and fires of earth (Huub Oosterhuis) 280
Love which leads to awareness (Caryl Micklem, editor) 139
Love's as warm as tears (Terry Falla) 335

Make us healthy-minded (Terry Falla) 136
Maker of heaven and earth (Terry Falla) 37
Many lovely things (Christopher Wade) 134
Mary's song (Luke 1:46-55) 201
Mercy and freedom are his gifts (Terry Falla) 26
Messengers of hope (Alan Gaunt) 161
More than we can measure or imagine
    (Ephesians 3:14-21) 278
My days are in your hand (Dietrich Bonhoeffer) 86

Never too poor to be generous (Ronald N. Ham) 159
New Year (Frank Rees) 221

Of driving clouds and open skies
    (Walter Rauschenbusch) 77
One Lord, one faith, one hope (Terry Falla) 234
Our call and commission (Terry Falla) 58
Our mission in the world (Terry Falla) 63
Our ultimate loyalty (Terry Falla) 172
Our utmost need (Terry Falla) 27
Ours were the sorrows he carried (Isaiah 52:13 — 53:12) 264
Out of the depths (Psalm 130) 84

Participants in evil (*An Order for Holy Communion*) 113
Patience that waits our returning (*The Worshipbook*) 73
Peace prayer of Francis of Assisi 150
Penitence (*Let's Worship*) 115
Pervade us, O God, with your presence
    (Caryl Micklem, editor) 33
Power (Caryl Micklem, editor) 109
Powers beyond our own (E. Milner-White) 282
Praise for the past and trust for the future (Alan Gaunt) 39
Praise him, all creation (Psalm 96) 22
Put your name upon us (Anonymous) 104

Rebellion (Bruce Prewer) 92
Recognizing the bonds (*Forms of Prayer for
    Jewish Worship*) 75
Redemptive suffering (Alan Gaunt) 168
Risen and still with you (Terry Falla) 52
Robert Louis Stevenson's Christmas Day Prayer 218

Shadows of fear (Caryl Micklem, editor) 253
Shafts of trust (Psalm 13) 89

359

Sharing (Jane Dyson) 134
Sounds of the Sacrament (Norman C. Habel) 190
Step into joy (a revised and enlarged version of a
  meditation composed by Peter Dyson, Darren French,
  Lynette French, Nerise Radford, Carol Summers and
  Susan Summers) 338
Steps marking our way (Caryl Micklem, editor) 119
Strength to comfort (2 Corinthians 1:3-7) 303
Summons to praise (Psalm 117) 21
Surprised by joy (Ian Hansen) 212

Take fire (*Living: Liturgical Style*) 116
Temptation (Athol Gill) 244
Tensed against tenderness (Anonymous) 110
Testing the promise by living the hope (Terry Falla) 25
Thanks for our heritage (Richard Jones, editor) 74
That dreams may be dreamt (*Let's Worship*) 121
The blessing of a child (Terry Falla) 292
The call of freedom has been sounded (Terry Falla) 21
The centre of the mystery of the Christ (Paul Tillich) 262
The commitment of the community (Terry Falla) 298
The community of grace (Terry Falla) 61
The cosmic Christ (Colossians 1:13-23) 44
The cost of discipleship (Caryl Micklem, editor) 241
The darkness is never so distant (Terry Falla) 254
The divine discontent (Anonymous) 122
The earth is yours (Terry Falla) 80
The goad of the promised future (Terry Falla) 66
The grace unspeakable (Graeme Garrett) 215
The immense longing (Terry Falla) 29
The insatiable desire (Meredith Butler) 202
The Lord's Prayer (adapted from the ICET version) 2
The meaning of providence (Romans 8:31-39) 48
The morning sun from heaven (*Forms of Prayer for
  Jewish Worship*) 232
The new commandment (Terry Falla) 251
The open church (Alan Marr) 288
The pledge of the Spirit (Pauline Webb, editor) 193
The promise of your presence (Terry Falla) 123
The rainbow of our future (Athol Gill) 208
The rhythm of community (Terry Falla) 154
The safest response to the surprising God?
  (Bruce Rumbold) 266
The scandal of grace (Terry Falla) 178
The simplicity of the carefree life (Marita Monro) 238
The thanksgiving (*An Australian Prayer Book*) 186
The threshold (Terry Falla) 257
The times we talk too much (Jo Carr and
  Imogene Sorley) 108
The true wilderness (Judith Jones) 242
The unexpected at every turn (Athol Gill) 233
The unquenchable hope (Terry Falla) 149
The wind of the Spirit (Terry Falla) 283
The Word was made flesh (Terry Falla) 127
There is a new world (Terry Falla and Judith Jones) 43
Things that make me sad (Lynette Falla) 87
Though the mountains may depart (Terry Falla) 28
Through the flames of heaven (Norman C. Habel) 276
To know God is to do justice (Edmund S.P. Jones, editor) 126

To make your purpose our purpose (Huub Oosterhuis) 35
To receive your gift (Karl Barth). 206
To the end (Helder Camara) 258
To your safe keeping (Bruce Rumbold) 304
Tomorrows filled with promise (Terry Falla) 200
Transformed nonconformist (Terry Falla). 322

Using our gifts (Terry Falla) 159

Valley of the shadow (Graeme Garrett) . . . . , 306
Venturing the harder road (Alan Gaunt) 164
Vision and mirage (Ronald C.D. Jasper, editor) 246

We are your family (Gwen Summers) 180
We commit ourselves to live in love (Alan Gaunt) 160
We do not take an untravelled way (Terry Falla). 69
We give you what we are (Anonymous) 106
We share his peace (*The Alternative Services Book 1980*) 182
Whatsoever you do (Mother Teresa of Calcutta) 153
When in prison you came to my cell (Anonymous) 145
When little is left (Ernest T. Campbell) 256
When the seas rage and mountains fall (Psalm 46). 49
Where many paths and errands meet (Karl Barth) 30
Where the Spirit of the Lord is, there is freedom
   (*Praise in All Our Days*). 236
Where your treasure is (Terry Falla) 155
Who takes away the sin of the world (Ernest A. Payne and
   Stephen F. Winward). 260
Widely as his mercy flows (Ernest A. Payne and
   Stephen F. Winward). 34
With no sense of compulsion (Ronald N. Ham) 158
With what gifts shall we come before him? (Terry Falla) 152
Worship without pretence (Romans 12:1,2,9-13) 24

Year's end (Karl Barth) 220
You are accepted (Terry Falla). 228
You have met us in your Son (*An Order for
   Holy Communion*) 189
You shall know the truth (Dietrich Bonhoeffer) 102
Your love is strong enough (Caryl Micklem, editor) 72
Your love is stronger than death (Bruce Rumbold) 308
Your word and your truth in our midst
   (Thorwald Lorenzen) 25
Yours is the kingdom (Ronald N. Ham) 160

AUTHORS AND SOURCES

*Most of the titles of the prayers and
readings were provided by the editor.*

A New Catechism
> Lines 32-35 of 'The unquenchable hope' adapted from *A
> New Catechism,* The Seabury Press, 1969, copyright 1967,
> 1969 by Herder and Herder, Inc. Used by permission.

Abrahams, Israel
> See Forms of Prayer for Jewish Worship.

An Australian Prayer Book
> 'The thanksgiving' from *An Australian Prayer Book,*
> 1978, Anglican Information Office (AIO Press), copyright
> 1978 by The Church of England in Australia Trust
> Corporation. Reprinted by permission.

An Order for Holy Communion

'Brought together to break bread', 'Do this remembering me', 'Given for the life of the world', 'Participants in evil', 'You have met us in your Son' adapted from *An Order for Holy Communion, Alternative Services Series 3*, Cambridge University Press, Oxford University Press, and SPCK, copyright 1971, 1973 by The Registrars of the Provinces of Canterbury and York. Used by permission.

Annals

Several quotations from the meditation 'Step into Joy' are from *Annals, A Journal of Current Affairs, Catechetics and the Media*, published by Chevalier Press, Kensington, N.S.W. From the March issue of *Annals '76:* the first paragraph on p. 338, the last on p. 339, the first and third on p. 342, the last on p 347, as well as other passages cited in the index under the names of their authors. Reprinted by permission. 'Blindness' was adapted from the same source. Used by permission.

Anonymous

The following prayers have been adapted from material the editor has been unable to trace to its source: 'A litany for the Lucky Country', 'Children learn what they live', 'Come away', 'Jesus', 'Put your name upon us', 'Tensed against tenderness', 'The divine discontent', 'We give you what we are', 'When in prison you came to my cell'.

Auden, W.H.

Quotation in 'Love which leads to awareness' from 'Another Time' and verses in 'Step into joy' from 'In Memory of W.B. Yeats' in *Collected Shorter Poems 1927-1957*, Faber and Faber Ltd., 1969, copyright 1966 by W.H. Auden. Reprinted by permission.

Augustine, of Hippo

Quotation on p. 117 from St Augustine's Confessions, VII, xxi, translated by C.S. Lewis in *Surprised by Joy*, Collins Fontana Books, 1959, copyright 1955 by C.S. Lewis. Reprinted by permission.

Baillie, John

'Forbid!', adapted from *A Diary of Private Prayer*, Oxford University Press, 1953. Used by permission.

Baptist Confession of 1646

Excerpt quoted in 'A taste of sawdust and a thirst for truth'.

Barrett, Graeme

Quotation in 'The threshold' from 'Apartheid: The Closing Phases?', *The Age*, Saturday, May 17, 1980. Reprinted by permission of *The Age*.

Barth, Karl

'He is one of us', 'To receive your gift', 'Year's end' adapted from *Selected Prayers by Karl Barth*, translated by Keith R. Crim, John Knox Press, copyright 1965 by M.E. Bratcher. Used by permission. 'Where many paths and errands meet' slightly adapted from *Congremur*, edited by the Youth Department, World Council of Churches, Geneva, revised edition 1967, copyright 1967 by World Council of Churches, Geneva. Used by permission.

Bonhoeffer, Dietrich
> Quotation on p. 248, 'You shall know the truth', from *The Cost of Discipleship*, copyright 1959 by SCM Press. Reprinted by permission.
> Quotation in 'Step into joy' from the May issue of *Annals '72*. Stanzas 2-3 of the prayer on p. 353 are based on a quotation in the June issue of *Annals '76*. 'My days are in your hand' adapted from *Congremur* (see Karl Barth for details). Used by permission.

Boyaxhiu, Mother Teresa
> 'Whatsoever you do' from *Something Beautiful for God* by Malcolm Muggeridge, Collins, 1971, copyright 1971 by The Mother Teresa Committee. Reprinted by permission.

Brandt, Leslie F.
> 'Eternal God and mortal man' adapted from *Good Lord, Where Are You? Prayers for the Twentieth Century based on the Psalms*, copyright 1967 by Concordia Publishing House. Used by permission.

Brockelsby, Joan
> Excerpt in 'Gossip' from 'Jesus weeps over Jerusalem', and the poem in 'Step into joy' from *Step into Joy, Poems*, Belton Books, copyright 1969 by Joan Brockelsby. Reprinted by permission.

Buchan, John
> Excerpt in 'Fortitude' from *Mr Standfast*, quoted by C.H. Dodd in *The Meaning of Paul for Today*, Collins Fontana Books, 1958, copyright by Cambridge University Press. Reprinted by permission.

Burke, Edmund
> Quotation in 'Courage to change'.

Butler, Meredith
> 'The insatiable desire'.

Calvin, John
> Quotation on p. 151.

Camara, Helder
> Quotation on p. 314, 'Come, Lord', 'To the end', from *The Desert is Fertile*, Sheed and Ward, English translation copyright 1974 by Orbis Books. Reprinted by permission. Quotation on p. 202 spoken by Helder Camara on an ABC television documentary.

Campbell, Ernest T.
> Stanzas 9-12, 14-16 of 'For our city and ourselves', 'When little is left', adapted from *Where Cross the Crowded Ways, Prayers of a City Pastor*, Association Press, copyright 1973 by Ernest T. Campbell. Used by permission.

Carr, Jo and Sorley, Imogene
> 'Longing for tomorrow and losing today', 'The times we talk too much', adapted from *Bless This Mess & Other Prayers*, copyright 1969 by Abingdon Press. Used by permission.

Carter, Paul
> The music for 'Search for the Infant' from *Carols for Children*, copyright 1972 by High-Fye Music Ltd. Used by permission.

Coventry Cathedral Pamphlets

'Father, forgive' copyright by the Provost and Chapter of Coventry Cathedral. Reprinted by permission.

Davies, Adele

'Happiness is . . .' rewritten by the author for responsive use from a meditation originally published by Clifford Press.

Dyson, Jane

'Sharing'.

Dyson, Peter and others

'Step into joy' is a revised and enlarged version of a meditation composed by Peter Dyson, Darren French, Lynette French, Nerise Radford, Carol Summers, and Susan Summers.

Eliot, T.S.

Quotation on p. 199 from *The Family Reunion,* copyright 1963 by Faber and Faber Ltd. Reprinted by permission. Verse on p. 301 from 'Little Gidding' in *Collected Poems 1909-1962,* Faber and Faber Ltd, copyright 1963 by T.S. Eliot. Reprinted by permission.

Faber, F.W.

Verse on p. 263 from *The Australian Hymn Book,* 1977.

Falla, Berris

Quotation in 'Gossip'.

Falla, Daniel, Jeremy, Matthew and Terry

'Fun times'.

Falla, Lynette

'Things that make me sad'.

Falla, Terry

Quotations on pp. 57 and 271, the prayer on p. 353 (stanzas 2,3 based on words of Dietrich Bonhoeffer), 'A letter not written with ink', 'A people on trial', 'A taste of sawdust and a thirst for truth', 'A world in which faith comes hard' (stanzas 1-3: Alan Gaunt), 'Acclaim with joy the depths of his love' (response: Alan Gaunt), 'Against the wind', 'Alive!' (based on anonymous material), 'Alpha and Omega', 'Belonging', 'Between already and not yet' (source material: John H. Westerhoff), 'Beyond what the silent stars tell', 'Choices' (stanzas 4-7: Caryl Micklem), 'Christmastide profiles' (based on a litany by Alec Yale), 'Courage to change', 'Doing the truth' (stanza 4 of the prayer: Martin Luther King), 'Emmanuel' (sources: Mark Link, Graeme Garrett), 'Enough!' (stanzas 3 and 5: Alan Marr), 'Fortitude', 'God saw all that he had made' (based on an anonymous prayer), 'Gossip', 'He is hidden' (lines 8-11: C.S. Lewis), 'Induction of elders or deacons', 'Induction of teachers or leaders', 'Just as we are' (stanzas 1-4: *The Alternative Service Book 1980*), 'Let the winds of the Spirit', 'Liberty to the oppressed' (based on an anonymous litany), 'Light of the world' (prose excerpt: Werner and Lotte Pelz), 'Love's as warm as tears', 'Make us healthy-minded' (based on an anonymous prayer), 'Maker of heaven and earth', 'Mercy and freedom are his gifts' (response: Caryl Micklem), 'One Lord, one faith, one hope', 'Our call and commission' (phrases from a sermon by Helmut Thielicke are used in the eleventh stanza), 'Our mission in the world', 'Our ultimate loyalty' (source material: *Service of the Newark Free Synagogue*), 'Our utmost need' (sources: *Forms of Prayer for Jewish Worship*, Paul Tillich), 'Powers beyond our own' (prayer: Eric Milner-White), 'Risen and still with you', 'Testing the promise by living the hope' (sources: Werner and Lotte Pelz, Brother Roger Schutz), 'The blessing of a child', 'The call of freedom has been sounded' (lines 1-11: Ernst Käsemann), 'The commitment of the community', 'The community of grace', 'The darkness is never so distant' (stanzas 4-7: Hans Lilje), 'The earth is yours' (stanzas 1-2: *The Worshipbook, Services*), 'The goad of the promised future' (based on a prayer by George Moot in the first edition of this book, entitled *A Book of Responsive Prayers and Readings*, printed in 1976 for the use of the Rosanna Baptist Church), 'The immense longing', 'The new commandment', 'The promise of your presence' (stanzas 1-3: adapted from an anonymous Jewish prayer; stanza 4: Alan Gaunt), 'The rhythm of community' (based on a prayer in *Forms of Prayer for Jewish Worship*), 'The scandal of grace', 'The threshold', 'The unquenchable hope' (lines 5, 27-30: Karl Rahner; lines 32-35: *A New Catechism*), 'The wind of the Spirit' (source material: James S. Stewart), 'The Word was made flesh' (based on an anonymous prayer), 'Though the mountains may depart', 'Tomorrows filled with promise' (stanza 4: *Forms of Prayer for Jewish Worship*), 'Transformed nonconformist', 'Using our gifts' (based on a prayer in *Contemporary Prayers for Public Worship*, edited by Caryl Micklem), 'We do not take an untravelled way' (second last stanza: Alan Gaunt), 'Where your treasure is', 'With what gifts shall we come before him?' (paraphrase of selections from Isaiah chapter 58 based on the *Jerusalem Bible* translation), 'You are accepted' (prose excerpt: Paul Tillich).

Falla, Terry, and Jones, Judith

'There is a new world' (several phrases are from the *New English Bible* and *The Jerusalem Bible*).

Falla, Terry, Jones, Judith and O'Brien, Rex

'Every part of our life'.

Farjeon, Eleanor

Words of the hymn 'Morning has broken' from *The Children's Bells*, copyright by David Higham Associates. Reprinted by permission.

Forms of Prayer for Jewish Worship

Stanzas 1-4 of 'Our utmost need', 'Recognizing the bonds', the fourth stanza of 'Tomorrows filled with promise', adapted from *Forms of Prayer for Jewish Worship*, edited by the Assembly of Rabbis of the Reform Synagogues of Great Britain, copyright 1977 by the Reform Synagogues of Great Britain. Used by permission. The first poem on p. 227 by Israel Abrahams and the second by Levi Yitzchak are from the same source. Reprinted by permission.

Francis of Assisi

'Peace prayer of Francis of Assisi'.

French, Darren
  See Dyson, Peter.

French, Lynette
  See Dyson, Peter.

Fromm, Eric
  Quotations in 'Step into joy' from the May issue of
  Annals '74.

Frost, Brian
  'Bread with laughter' slightly adapted from *Living:*
  Liturgical Style (see below), copyright by Stainer and Bell
  Ltd. Reprinted by permission.

Fynn
  Excerpt in 'Step into joy' from *Mister God this is Anna,*
  William Collins Sons & Co. Ltd. 1974, copyright 1974 by
  Fynn. Reprinted by permission.

Garrett, Graeme
  The prayer in 'Emmanuel', 'Hallelujah for the Christ-
  child!', 'The grace unspeakable', 'Valley of the shadow'.

Gaunt, Alan
  Stanzas 1-3 of 'A world in which faith comes hard', the
  response in 'Acclaim with joy the depths of his love',
  'Here and now', 'Messengers of hope', 'Praise for the past
  and trust for the future', 'Redemptive suffering', the last
  stanza of 'The promise of your presence', 'Venturing the
  harder road', 'We commit ourselves to live in love', the
  second last stanza of 'We do not take an untravelled way'
  adapted from *New Prayers for Worship,* John Paul the
  Preacher's Press, copyright 1975 by Alan Gaunt. Used by
  permission.

Gill, Athol
  'A surprising start', 'Breath of our life', 'Temptation',
  'The rainbow of our future', 'The unexpected at every
  turn'.

Griffin, Graeme
  'Forgiveness'.

Griffiths, David
  'Because you believe in us', adapted from prayers by
  W.B.J. Martin in *Acts of Worship,* copyright 1960 by
  Abingdon Press. Used by permission. 'For our city and
  ourselves' stanzas 9-12, 14-16 are adapted from Ernest T.
  Campbell (see above).

Griffiths, David and O'Brien, Rex
  'Limb and mind in harmony'.

Habel, Norman C.
  'Confessions at the empty tomb', 'Dreams for celebration'
  (slightly adapted), 'Healings from the empty tomb',
  'Sounds of the Sacrament', 'Through the flames of
  heaven' from *Interrobang? Prayers and Shouts,*
  Lutterworth Press, 1970, copyright 1969 by Fortress Press.
  Reprinted by permission.

Ham, Ronald N.
  'Counterfeit?', 'Never too poor to be generous', 'With no
  sense of compulsion', 'Yours is the kingdom'.

Hammarskjöld, Dag
> Quotations in 'Surprised by joy' and on p. 219 from
> *Markings,* translated by W.H.Auden and Leif Sjoberg,
> Faber and Faber Ltd., 1964, copyright 1964 by Alfred A.
> Knopf Inc. and Faber and Faber Ltd. Reprinted by
> permission.

Hansen, Ian
> 'Surprised by joy'.

House of the Gentle Bunyip
> 'Granting of forgiveness' from the House of the Gentle
> Bunyip Christian community, Melbourne. The second
> stanza is from *The Daily Office Revised,* edited by Ronald
> C.D. Jasper (see below).

ICET
> Gloria in excelsis from *Prayers We Have In Common,*
> copyright 1970, 1971, 1975 by the International
> Consultation on English Texts (ICET). Reprinted by
> permission. 'The Lord's Prayer' backing the half-title
> page, except for lines 2 and 9, is that published by ICET,
> 1970.

Jasper, Ronald C.D.
> The second stanza of 'Granting of forgiveness', 'Vision
> and mirage' adapted from *The Daily Office Revised, With
> Other Prayers and Services,* edited by Ronald C.D. Jasper,
> SPCK, copyright 1978 by The Joint Liturgical Group.
> Used by permission.

Jeremias, Joachim
> Quotation in 'The scandal of grace' from *New Testament
> Theology,* Volume One, translated by John Bowden, SCM
> Press Ltd, copyright 1971 by Joachim Jeremias. Reprinted
> by permission.

Jones, Edmund S.P.
> 'To know God is to do justice' from *Worship and Wonder,*
> edited by Edmund S.P. Jones, Galliard Ltd, 1971.
> Reprinted by permission.

Jones, Judith
> 'The true wilderness'. See also Falla, Terry.

Jones, Richard
> 'Thanks for our heritage' adapted from *Worship for
> Today, Suggestions and Ideas,* edited by Richard Jones,
> Epworth Press, copyright 1968 by Richard Jones. Used by
> permission.

Käsemann, Ernst
> Quotations on pp. 224,235 (lines 7-10 are the editor's based
> on material by Ernst Käsemann), and 236 from *Jesus
> Means Freedom,* copyright 1969 by SCM Press Ltd.
> Reprinted by permission. Lines 1-11 of 'The call of
> freedom has been sounded' adapted from the same source.
> Used by permission.

Kempis, Thomas à
> Quotation in 'Gossip' from *The Imitation of Christ,* II, v.

King, Martin Luther

Quotations in 'A letter not written with ink' from source
unknown. Quotations in 'Transformed Nonconformist'
from the sermon 'Transformed Nonconformist' in
Strength to Love, Collins Fontana Books, 1969. Reprinted
by permission of Laurence Pollinger Ltd. The content of
the prayer on pp. 323,324 and of the last prayer on p. 325
are derived from the same sermon; the content of the
fourth stanza of the prayer on p. 249 is derived from the
sermon 'Tough Minds and Tender Hearts' in the same
book. Used by permission.

Küng, Hans

Quotation in 'Step into joy' from the March issue of
Annals '71.

Langmead, Ross

Music and words of the song composed for use in this
book as part of the meditation 'Step into joy', copyright
1981 by Ross Langmead.

Leader's Guide to *Move Man!*

'Crucified risen one!', 'Delivered to death for our
misdeeds', 'I have betrayed' from Leader's Guide to *Move
Man! Together with extra resources for worship.*
Presbyterian, Methodist, Congregational Boards of
Christian Education, Melbourne, 1969. Reprinted by
permission of the Joint Board of Christian Education,
Melbourne.

Let's Worship

'But not alone', 'Failed', 'Penitence', 'That dreams may be
dreamt' adapted from *Let's Worship, A Risk Book,* WCC
Publications Office, Geneva, 1978. Used by permission.

Lewis, C.S.

Quotation on p. 223 from *The Four Loves,* Collins
Fontana Books, 1963, copyright 1960 by C.S. Lewis.
Reprinted by permission. 'Footnote to all prayers', the
poem 'Love's as Warm as Tears' from *Poems,* edited by
Walter Hooper, Geoffrey Bles Ltd, 1964, copyright 1964 by
the Executors of the Estate of C.S. Lewis. Reprinted by
permission of William Collins Sons & Co. Ltd. Lines 8-11
of 'He is hidden' adapted from *A Grief Observed,* Faber
and Faber Ltd., 1961, copyright 1961 by C.S. Lewis. Used
by permission. See Augustine for a quotation from C.S.
Lewis's *Surprised by Joy.*

Lilje, Hans

Quotation on p. 97 from *The Valley of the Shadow,*
translated by Olive Wyon, copyright 1950 by Fortress
Press. Reprinted by permission. Stanzas 6-9 of 'The
darkness is never so distant' adapted from the same
source. Used by permission.

Link, Mark

'Song of an "Unpoet" ' in 'Emmanuel' and the four-line
verse heading Robert Louis Stevenson's Christmas Day
Prayer from *The Merriest Christmas Book,* copyright 1974
by Argus Communications.

Living: Liturgical Style
> 'Take fire' adapted from *Living: Liturgical Style, Risk,*
> Volume 5, Number 1, 1969, WCC Publications Office,
> Geneva. Used by permission.

Lorenzen, Thorwald
> 'Your word and your truth in our midst'.

Lowe, Daphne
> Poem in 'Step into joy'. Used by permission of the author.

Lowell, James Russell
> Excerpt in 'Transformed Nonconformist' from 'Stanzas on
> Freedom' in *The Poetical Works of James Russell Lowell,*
> by William Michael Rossetti, Ward, Lock & Co. Ltd.

Loyola, Ignatius
> 'A prayer of Ignatius Loyola'.

Macdonald, Mary
> Verse on p. 209 from *The Australian Hymn Book,* 1977.

Macquarrie, John
> Quotation on p. 315 from *New Directions in Theology
> Today,* Volume 3, *God and Secularity,* Lutterworth Press,
> 1968, copyright 1966 by W.L. Jenkins. Reprinted by
> permission. Footnote on p. viii.

Marr, Alan
> 'The open church'. Stanzas 3 and 5 of 'Enough!' are
> derived from an unpublished sermon by Alan Marr.

Martin, W.B.J.
> See Griffiths, David.

Merton, Thomas
> Quotations in 'Transformed Nonconformist' from *He Is
> Risen,* copyright 1975 by Argus Communications.
> Reprinted by permission.

Micklem, Caryl
> 'Beyond all pretence', 'Free to forget our pride', 'Go with us,
> Lord', 'Love which leads to awareness', the response in
> 'Mercy and freedom are his gifts', 'Pervade us, O God, with
> your presence', 'Shadows of fear', 'Steps marking our way',
> 'The cost of discipleship', 'Your love is strong enough'
> adapted from *Contemporary Prayers for Public Worship,*
> edited by Caryl Micklem, copyright 1967 by SCM Press Ltd.
> Used by permission. 'Stanzas 4-7 of 'Choices' and 'Power'
> from *More Contemporary Prayers,* edited by Caryl Micklem,
> copyright 1970 by SCM Press Ltd. Reprinted by permission.

Miles, Roy
> Quotation in 'A taste of sawdust and a thirst for truth'.

Milner-White, Eric
> Prayer in 'Powers beyond our own' adapted from *My God
> my Glory,* SPCK, 1967, copyright 1954, 1967 by The
> Friends of York Minster. Used by permission.

Miskotte, Kornelis H.
> Quotation on p. 67 from *The Roads of Prayer,* translated
> by John W. Doberstein, copyright 1968 by Sheed and
> Ward. Reprinted by permission.

Moltmann, Jürgen
Quotation in 'The goad of the promised future' and
quotation (slightly adapted) on p. 313 from *Theology of
Hope*, translated by James V. Leitch, copyright 1967 by
SCM Press Ltd. Reprinted by permission.

Munroe, Marita
'The simplicity of the carefree life'.

Narkeiwicz, Simon
'God gives'.

Newton, John
Verse in 'You are accepted' from the hymn 'Amazing
Grace'.

Niemöller, Martin
Quotation in 'The darkness is never so distant'.

Niebuhr, Reinhold
Quotations in 'Courage to change' and 'Transformed
Nonconformist' from *Courage to Change, An Introduction
to the Life and Thought of Reinhold Niebuhr* by June
Bingham, Charles Scribner's Sons, 1961.

Norbet, Gregory
Music and words of song in 'Step into joy' copyright by
Gregory Norbet. Used by permission.

Nouwen, Henri J.M.
Quotation on p. 287 from *Reaching Out*, William Collins
Sons & Co. Ltd., 1976, copyright 1975 by Henri J.M.
Nouwen. Reprinted by permission. Footnote on p. 8.

O'Brien, Rex
'Grass by the roadside' adapted from *Prayers of Life* by
Michel Quoist, translated by Anne Marie de Commaile
and Agnes Mitchell Forsyth, Logos Books, 1966, copyright
translation 1963 by Sheed and Ward. Used by permission.
Quotation on p. 314. See also Falla, Terry; Griffiths,
David.

Oosterhuis, Huub
'Attune us to your silence', 'Lord of the winds and fires of
earth', 'To make your purpose our purpose' adapted from
Your Word is Near, Contemporary Christian Prayers,
translated by N.D. Smith, Paulist Press, 1968, copyright
1968 by The Missionary Society of St Paul the Apostle in
the State of New York. Used by permission.

Pasternak, Boris
Verse on p. 293 from *Pasternak Fifty Poems*, chosen and
translated by Lydia Pasternak Slater, copyright 1963 by
George Allen & Unwin Ltd. Reprinted by permission.

Payne, Ernest and Winward, Stephen F.
'Widely as his mercy flows', 'Who takes away the sin of
the world' adapted from *Orders and Prayers for Church
Worship*, compiled by Ernest A. Payne and Stephen F.
Winward, copyright 1960 by The Carey Kingsgate Press
Ltd. Used by permission.

Pelz, Werner and Lotte
Quotation in 'Testing the promise by living the hope' and
prose excerpt in 'Light of the world' from *God Is No more,*
Penguin Books Ltd, 1968, copyright 1963 by Werner and
Lotte Pelz. Reprinted by permission.

Powell, John
Quotation in 'A taste of sawdust and a thirst for truth'
from *Why Am I Afraid to Tell You Who I Am?* Argus
Communications, 1969. Reprinted by permission.

Praise in All Our Days
'Jesus our Lord', 'Where the Spirit of the Lord is, there is
freedom' from *Praise in All Our Days, Common Prayer at
Taizé,* translated by Emily Chisholm, Faith Press Ltd,
1975, copyright 1975 by Les Presses de Taize. Used by
permission.

Prewer, Bruce
'Forsaken?', 'Good Friday', 'Holiness', 'Rebellion' from
Australian Psalms, copyright 1979 by Lutheran
Publishing House. Reprinted by permission.

Quoist, Michel
See O'Brien, Rex.

Radford, Nerise
See Dyson, Peter.

Rahner, Karl
Lines 25, 27-30 of 'The unquenchable hope' adapted from
The Shape of the Church to Come, copyright translation
1974 by SPCK. Used by permission.

Rauschenbusch, Walter
'Of driving clouds and open skies' adapted from *The
Meaning of Prayer,* by Harry Emerson Fosdick, SCM
Press Ltd., 1915.

Rees, Frank
'New Year'.

Rinder, Walter
Quotations in 'Step into joy' from *This Time Called Life,*
Celestial Arts, 1971, copyright 1971 by Walter Rinder.
Reprinted by permission of Celestial Arts.

Rumbold, Bruce D.
'A gift of grace', 'Footprints on the shore', 'Glimpses of a
winding road', 'Go well, stay well', 'Letting go', 'The
safest response to the surprising God?', 'To your safe
keeping', 'Your love is stronger than death'.

Ruskin, John
Quotation in 'A taste of sawdust and a thirst for truth'.

Schutz, Brother Roger
The prayer in 'Testing the promise by living the hope' is
adapted from material in *The Rule of Taize,* copyright
1968 by Les Presses de Taizé. Used by permission.

Schweizer, Eduard
Quotation in 'Beyond what the silent stars tell' from *The Good News According to Matthew*, translated by David E. Green, SPCK, 1976, copyright 1975, by John Knox Press. Reprinted by permission. The content of the fifth and sixth stanzas of the prayer in 'Doing the truth' is derived from the same source.

Service of the Newark Free Synagogue
Stanzas 1-6 of 'Our ultimate loyalty' are based on a prayer from the *Service of the Newark Free Synagogue*, 1924; the prayer is in *The Wisdom of Israel*, edited by Lewis Browne, Four Square Books, 1962.

Short, Robert L.
The quotation in 'Step into joy' from *The Parables of Peanuts*, Collins Fontana Books, 1969, copyright 1968 by United Feature Syndicate Inc. Reprinted by permission.

Solzhenitsyn, Alexander
Prayer in 'Against the wind' translated and published by the Centre for the Study of Religion and Communism. Reprinted by permission.

Stevenson, Robert Louis
See Link, Mark.

Stewart, James S
Quotation in 'The wind of the Spirit' from *The Wind of the Spirit*, Hodder and Stoughton, 1968, copyright 1968 by James S. Stewart. Reprinted by permission. Phrases from the same source are used in the prayer that follows the quotation.

Stewart, Michelle
'Find your love' from *Made it Sixteen*, Treking, Warrandyte, Victoria, copyright 1979 by Michelle Jean Stewart. Reprinted by permission.

Summers, Gwen
'We are your family'.

Summers, Carol
See Dyson, Peter.

Summers, Susan
See Dyson, Peter.

Taylor, John V.
Quotation on p. 277 from *The Go-Between God*, copyright 1972 by SCM Press Ltd. Reprinted by permission. Footnote on p. 8.

Teilhard de Chardin, Pierre
Quotation in 'Step into joy' from November issue of *Annals '73*.

Boyaxhiu, Mother Teresa of Calcutta
See Boyaxhiu.

The Alternative Service Book 1980
'We share his peace' adapted from *The Alternative Service Book 1980*, Cambridge University Press, William Clowes Ltd, SPCK, copyright 1980 by The Central Board of Finance of the Church of England. Used by permission. Stanzas 1-4 of 'Just as we are' are based on a prayer from the same source.

The Baptist Hymn Book
Verse in 'Our ultimate loyalty' from hymn 362 in *The Baptist Hymn Book*, 1962; originally from the Anabaptist *Ausbund*, 16th cent., translated by E.A. Payne. Reprinted by permission.

The Worshipbook, Services
'In all things be our strength', 'Patience that waits our returning', stanzas 1-2 of 'The earth is yours' adapted from *The Worshipbook, Services*, prepared by the Joint Committee on Worship for Cumberland Presbyterian Church, Presbyterian Church in the United States, The United Presbyterian Church in the United States of America, copyright 1970 by The Westminster Press. Used by permission.

Tillich, Paul
Lines 15-16, 18 of 'Our utmost need', 'The centre of the mystery of the Christ', prose excerpt in 'You are accepted' from *The Shaking of the Foundations*, The Scribner Library, Lyceum Editions, copyright 1948 by Charles Scribner's Sons. Reprinted by permission.

Tolkien, J.R.R.
Quotation on p. 259 from *The Lord of the Rings*, copyright 1966 by George Allen & Unwin Ltd. Reprinted by permission.

Vann, Gerald
Quotation introducing the meditation 'Happiness is . . .' from *The Divine Pity*, Collins Fontana Books, 1956. Reprinted by permission.

Wade, Alan
'Life can begin again'.

Wade, Christopher
'Many lovely things'.

Ward, Roy
Words of the hymn 'Search for the Infant' from *Carols for Children* (see Paul Carter for details). Reprinted by permission.

Webb, Pauline
'In the stillness', 'The pledge of the Spirit' adapted from the appendix of prayers and meditations from the Bangkok Conference in *Salvation Today*, SCM Press Ltd, 1974, copyright by World Council of Churches, Geneva. Used by permission.

Westerhoff, John H.
The content of stanzas 1-10 of 'Between already and not yet' is derived from material in chapter two of *Will Our Children have Faith?*, Dove Communications, copyright 1976 by The Seabury Press. Used by permission.

Whittier, John Greenleaf
Verse on p. 155 from *The Poetical Works of John Greenleaf Whittier*, Ward, Lock, & Co.

Williams, Daniel Day
Quotation on p. 41 from *The Spirit and the Forms of Love*, Library of Constructive Theology, James Nisbet, 1968, copyright 1968 by Daniel Day Williams. Reprinted by permission.

Yitzchak, Levi of Berditchev
    See *Forms of Prayer for Jewish Worship.*

To the above acknowledgements I would like to add my
indebtedness to a few persons and sources for distinctive phrases
I have used as titles: 'Risen and still with you', 'The immense
longing', 'The unquenchable hope' are titles in *A New Catechism;*
'The darkness is never so distant' is from a poem by W.H. Auden;
'The cost of discipleship' is the title of a book by Dietrich
Bonhoeffer, and 'The simplicity of the carefree life' is a heading in
that book; 'Step into joy' is the title of a book of poems by Joan
Brockelsby; 'Tomorrows filled with promise' is from a poem by
Edward Cunningham; 'Lord of the winds and fires of earth' is
from a prayer by Norman C. Habel; 'Surprised by joy' is the title
of a book by C.S. Lewis; 'Widely as his mercy flows' is from a
hymn by H.F. Lyte; 'Go well, stay well' is the title of a book by
Hannah Stanton; 'My days are in your hand' is from *The
Jerusalem Bible* translation of Psalm 31; 'Venturing the harder
road' is the title of a sermon by Helmut Thielicke; 'Where many
paths and errands meet' is from a poem by J.R.R. Tolkien;
'Recognizing the bonds' is used as a heading by Jean Vanier; 'The
insatiable desire', used as the title and theme of the prayer by
Meredith Butler, is taken from Gerald Vann's book *The Divine
Pity;* 'Broken bones may joy' is the title of a book by Alan
Webster; 'The true wilderness' is the title of a book by H.A.
Williams.

SCRIPTURE PASSAGES

*Scripture passages set out in responsive form were arranged by the
editor. Several passages are the editor's translation or paraphrase.*

Genesis 1:31 128
Genesis 8:22 128
Exodus 16:9-21 233
Exodus 20:1-17 Selections .. **251**
Numbers 6:24-26 292
Job 9:11, cf. 23:8-9 88
Psalm 1:1-2 328
Psalm 8 81,352
Psalm 8:5 36
Psalm 13 89
Psalm 29 79
Psalm 30 Selections 71
Psalm 46 49
Psalm 51 Selections 85
Psalm 90 Paraphrase 96
Psalm 95:4,5 80
Psalm 96 22
Psalm 100 38,39
Psalm 103 50
Psalm 103:15,16 36
Psalm 117 21
Psalm 121 299
Psalm 130 84
Psalm 139 Selections 99
Psalm 148 Selections 82
Isaiah 6:3 320,321
Isaiah 40:12-14 37
Isaiah 42:5-7 23
Isaiah 43:1 28,29
Isaiah 44:2 28
Isaiah 44:6 37
Isaiah 44:21,22 28
Isaiah 44:24 37
Isaiah 52:13 — 53:12 264
Isaiah 54:4 28
Isaiah 54:7 28
Isaiah 54:8 28
Isaiah 54:10 28
Isaiah 55:6-9 28
Isaiah 58:2-11 Paraphrases
  of selections 152
Jeremiah 6:14,15 254,255
Jeremiah 22:16 126
Micah 6:1-8 94
Micah 6:8 344
Micah 7:18-20 98
Matthew 1:21-23 210
Matthew 2:1-12 224
Matthew 4:1-10 244
Matthew 5:3 (Luke 6:20) ... 328
Matthew 5:4 329
Matthew 5:5 330
Matthew 5:6 330
Matthew 5:7 331
Matthew 5:8 332
Matthew 5:9 332
Matthew 5:10-12
  (Luke 6:22-23) 333
Matthew 6:9-13 2,31

Matthew 6:14,15 317
Matthew 6:25-34 240
Matthew 6:26-30 347
Matthew 7:12 344
Matthew 7:24-27 248
Matthew 9:13b 95
Matthew 9:13c 19
Matthew 10:34 174
Matthew 23:23 95
Matthew 25:31-46 145
Matthew 25:35-46 153
Matthew 28 52
Mark 1:9-11 230
Mark 3:14 61
Mark 6:31 35
Mark 8:34 95
Mark 10:32 253
Mark 10:38 .... **241**
Mark 10:42-45 295
Luke 1:46-55 201
Luke 1:68-79 204
Luke 1:78 232
Luke 2:8-14 212
Luke 4:18 26,37
Luke 9 52
Luke 9:23 163
Luke 9:51 258
Luke 10:27 160
Luke 10:28 25
Luke 24:35 175
John 1:14 127
John 1:18 120
John 1:29 260
John 2:1-11 233
John 6:1-14 233
John 6:51 180
John 8:31,32 248
John 8:32 102
John 9:39-41 112,226
John 13:34 .... **251**
John 20:29 334
Acts 20:35 159
Romans 4:25 95,270
Romans 5:1 95
Romans 5:2-5 326
Romans 5:7,8 43
Romans 5:8 262
Romans 5:20 229
Romans 8:31-39 48
Romans 12:1,2 24
Romans 12:2a 322
Romans 12:2b 322
Romans 12:9-13 24
Romans 14:10-13 318
1 Corinthians 12:4-7 ... 294,296
1 Corinthians 12:27 294,296
1 Corinthians 13 335
2 Corinthians 1:3-7 303
2 Corinthians 3:3 125

2 Corinthians 3:17 238
2 Corinthians 5:5 193
2 Corinthians 5:15-21 43
2 Corinthians 5:18 229
2 Corinthians 5:19 229
2 Corinthians 6:4-10 326
2 Corinthians 7:10 83
Galatians 3:28 127
Ephesians 1:17-19 282
Ephesians 2:1-10 46
Ephesians 2:20 279
Ephesians 3:14-21 278
Ephesians 3:18 292
Ephesians 4:4-6 234
Philippians 1:9 292
Philippians 1:9,10 316
Philippians 1:10 234

Philippians 1:20 326
Philippians 2:1-5 Selections 234
Philippians 2:3-5 344
Philippians 4:8 319
Colossians 1:13-23 44
Colossians 1:13 94
1 Thessalonians 5:11-24
     Selections 234
2 Timothy 1:6 292,294,296
James 1:17 78
James 1:26 317
James 3:5 317
1 John 1:8-10 177
1 John 4:7-10 251
1 John 4:16-21 252
Revelation 4:1-3 208

ABOUT THE AUTHOR

Dr Terry Falla was born on Guernsey in the Channel Islands in 1940, but came to Australia at an early age, and has spent most of his life in Victoria. Following adult matriculation in 1961, he forged a distinguished academic record at the University of Melbourne, earning his BA (1966) and MA (1967) with First Class Honours, and his PhD (1972), specializing in the Hebrew and Syriac biblical and post-biblical languages. At the invitation of Professor Bruce Metzger, his doctoral work has become the basis of a lexicographical work, *A Key to the Peshitta Gospels*, now being prepared as a volume in the series *New Testament Tools and Studies* for publication by E.J. Brill (Leyden).

Dr Falla has served as lecturer (1971-80) in Old Testament Studies at Whitley College, University of Melbourne, minister of Baptist churches at Ashburton (associate, 1968-70) and Rosanna (1971-78), and is now a chaplain to La Trobe University. He is married to Berris, and has four children.